2009中国保险市场年报

ANNUAL REPORT OF CHINA INSURANCE MARKET 2009

目 录

Contents

壹

主席致辞

2009 年是新世纪以来我国经济发展最为困难的一年，也是保险业应对国际金融危机、迎接挑战、经受考验的一年。面对极为复杂的国内外经济金融环境，保险业深入实践科学发展观，认真贯彻落实党中央、国务院有关金融保险工作的要求，着力防范风险，进一步深化改革，加快发展方式转变，调整业务结构，扩大保险服务领域，服务经济社会发展全局，各项工作取得显著成绩。

保险业务发展好于预期

2009 年，全行业保费首次突破 1 万亿元①，达到 11137.3 亿元，同比增长 13.8%。财产险业务继续保持较快增长，实现保费 2875.8 亿元，同比增长 23.1%。人身险业务保费达 8261.5 亿元，在 2008 年增速较高的基础上同比增长 10.9%。全年赔付金额 3125.5 亿元。经营效益大幅提升，保险公司利润总额达到 845 亿元。财产险公司扭亏为盈，实现利润 72.4 亿元。人身险公司实现利润 708 亿元，业务价值显著提升。再保险业务承保质量明显改善。全行业实现投资收益 2141.7 亿元，收益率为 6.41%，比上年提高 4.5 个百分点。保险业整体实力明显增强，截至 2009 年年底，保险公司总资产突破 4 万亿元，达到 4.1 万亿元。净资产 4604.8 亿元，比上年年末增加 1441.8 亿元②。保险资金运用余额为 3.7 万亿元。

---

① 除特殊说明外，本年报中财务数据均是执行《企业会计准则解释第 2 号》后的审计数据。保费及赔付金额均为业务口径统计数据。

② 本年报中财务数据为同口径数据对比，2008 年财务数据根据变更后的会计政策进行了追溯调整。

行业风险得到有效防范

2009年，保险业把风险防范作为首要任务，积极采取措施，努力化解国际金融危机的冲击。对保险业风险状况实施动态监测和压力测试，制定风险应急预案，开展保险集团公司风险排查，不断完善风险防范机制。批准45家公司增资225亿元、10家公司发行次级债180亿元，积极改善偿付能力状况。督促公司提取足额现金准备，将万能险结算利率和分红险分红水平稳定在长期可持续水平，防范和控制新型保险产品退保风险。制定和调整保险资金管理制度，扩大资产配置空间，防范低利率带来的错配风险。截至2009年年底，偿付能力不达标的保险公司共8家，比年初减少5家，不达标公司的偿付能力关键指标较年初有明显改善。人身险公司退保率为3.54%，退保情况总体稳定。保险公司现金流保持充裕。保险资产配置较好地实现了安全性、流动性和收益性的平衡。风险跨境传递得到有效控制。

结构调整取得积极进展

2009年，保险业坚持把推动结构调整和应对国际金融危机、转变发展方式结合起来，增强行业的可持续发展能力。从财产险看，农业险、信用险、工程险等非车险业务分别同比增长21%、91.3%和31.6%；非寿险投资型产品投资余额为506.4亿元，较上年年末减少426.5亿元。从人身险看，标准保费同比增长19.5%，增速高于规模保费8.6个百分点；新单业务中，期交保费占比25.2%，同比上升5.4个百分点，其中10年期及以上保费占新单业务比重上升1.7个百分点；个人代理业务占比43.8%，同比上升1.8个百分点；银邮代理业务占比47.7%，同比下降1.2个百分点。从保险投资看，资产配置结构不断优化，投资管理水平逐步提高。

服务全局的能力逐步增强

2009年，保险业全力服务“保增长、保民生、保稳定”，充分发挥保险“经济助推器”的作用，大力发展出口信用保险，短期出口信用险累计承保额达902.7亿美元，同比增长122.6%。积极服务“三农”和参与社会保障体系建设，大力发展农业保险，保费达133.9亿元，提供风险保障3812亿元，同比增长59%；参保农户1.33亿户次，同比增长48%。稳步推进小额保险试点，小额保险保费达2.3亿元，为871万人提供风险保障1364亿元。切实发挥保险的社会风险管理功能，大力推动医疗、交通、教育以及环保等领域的责任保险发展，环境污染责任保险在8个省市试点、医疗责任保险在16个省区市的56个地市启动。医疗责任保险成为中央综治办建立平安医院的重要措施，在化解医患事故纠纷、分担医疗责任风险方面发挥了积极作用。指导有关公司做好婴幼儿奶粉事件患儿医疗赔偿基金管理工作。积极应对东北地区旱灾和部分地区雪灾，做好理赔服务，服务经济社会发展和人民生活。

保险监管工作成效显著

2009年，面对极为复杂的国内外经济金融环境，保险监管机构坚持“防风险、调结构、稳增长”的工作方针，扎实推进保险业又好又快发展。认真应对国际金融危机，不仅有效地防范了各种新的风险，而且积极化解历史遗留问题，完善防范风险的长效机制，积累了驾驭复杂形势的宝贵经验。以实施新修订的《保险法》为契机，不断健全保险监管制度体系，全面推进依法监管。着重加强对法人机构的监管，全面推行分类监管，强化偿付能力监管，完善保险公司治理监管，切实提高监管的有效性。出重拳加大市场行为监管力度，保险市场秩序逐步好转，财产险保费批退率为5%，同比下降2.3个百分点。应收保费率为3.1%，同比下降2.9个百分点。保险公司的业务和财务数据真实性进一步提高。人身险公司销售行为逐步规范，销售误导在一定程度上得到遏制。全年处理保险举报投诉5150件，保护被保险人利益工作进一步加强。

在发展形势极为复杂的情况下，2009年保险工作取得了积极进展，是近年来成绩较为显著的一年，是十六大以来保险业改革发展成果的集中体现。借此机会，我代表保监会向保险业全体干部职工和多年来一直关心支持中国保险业改革发展的社会各界人士及海内外朋友表示衷心的感谢！

2010年是保险业实施“十一五”规划的最后一年，也是应对国际金融危机的关键一年。保险业将继续深入落实科学发展观，全面贯彻中央经济工作会议精神，坚持转方式、调结构、防风险、促发展，更加注重转变发展方式，更加注重防范化解风险，更加注重夯实发展基础，更加注重增强服务能力，更加注重保护被保险人利益，努力促进保险业平稳较快发展，力争为经济社会的发展进步作出新的更大的贡献！

中国保险监督管理委员会主席 吴定富

2010年8月30日

贰

经济社会的进步和发展

- 经济社会取得新的进步和发展，保险市场发展的空间不断拓展
- 中国综合实力进一步增强，夯实了保险市场发展的基础
- 金融业持续安全健康发展，促进经济发展能力快速提升

2009年是新世纪以来我国经济发展最为困难的一年。在党中央、国务院的坚强领导下，中国人民从容应对国际金融危机冲击，在世界率先实现经济回升向好，改革开放和社会主义现代化建设取得新的重大成就。

经济社会的进步和发展

经济社会取得新的进步和发展，保险市场发展的空间不断拓展

成功应对国际金融危机

2009年，国际金融危机蔓延深入。我国政府及时调整宏观经济政策导向，实施积极的财政政策和适度宽松的货币政策，在扩大内需、振兴产业、发展科技、完善社会保障等方面出台了促进经济平稳较快发展的一揽子计划。中央政府公共投资9243亿元，比上年预算增加5038亿元，主要投向保障性住房、农村民生工程、社会事业投资、自主创新、结构调整、节能减排、生态建设、重大基础设施和灾后恢复重建。全社会固定资产投资增长30.1%，有效地弥补了外需下降的缺口。中国迅速走出经济增长的低谷，在世界率先实现经济回升向好，激发了全国人民的自信心和自豪感，提升了我国的国际地位和影响力。

新农村建设进一步加强

围绕稳粮、增收、强基础、重民生，惠农政策进一步强化。2009年中央财政用于“三农”的支出达7253亿元，比上年增加1298亿元，增长21.8%。粮食最低收购价大幅度提高。全国新增千亿斤粮食生产能力建设规划启动实施。农村水、电、路、气、房建设继续加强。农村教育、医疗、社保制度不断健全。农村体制创新取得新的突破。粮食生产连续6年实现增产。农民工就业快速回升。农民人均纯收入首次突破5000元大关。农业社会和谐稳定发展，为扩大内需、推动经济企稳向好提供了有力的基础支撑。

民生建设着力推进

在应对国际金融危机的困难情况下，坚持以人为本、民生优先，统筹兼顾、突出重点，实施更加积极的就业政策，大幅度增加全国教育支出，大力开展医药卫生体制改革，切实解决人民群众最关心、最直接、最现实的利益问题。2009年，中央财政用于就业、教育和医疗卫生的支出分别为426亿元、1981亿元和1277亿元，分别比上年增长59%、23.6%和49.5%。

社会保障体系加快完善

在320个县开展新型农村社会养老保险试点，推动我国社会保障制度建设迈出历史性步伐。城镇职工基本养老保险省级统筹普遍建立。养老和医疗保险转移接续办法陆续出台。企业退休人员基本养老金连续5年增加。城镇职工和城镇居民基本医疗保险参保4.01亿人，新型农村合作医疗制度覆盖8.3亿人。2009年，中央财政用于社会保障和就业的支出达2906亿元，比上年增长16.6%。全国社会保障基金积累达6927亿元，比上年增长44.2%。

中国综合实力进一步增强，夯实了保险市场发展的基础

国民经济形势总体回升向好

2009年，中国国内生产总值达33.5万亿元，比上年增长8.7%。全国财政收入达6.85万亿元，比上年增长11.7%；国家外汇储备达到2.4万亿美元。

改革开放继续深化

中国把深化改革开放作为应对国际金融危机的强大动力，努力消除体制障碍，不断提高对外开放水平。地方政府机构改革有序开展，事业单位分类改革试点稳步进行。资源性产品价格、财税体制、金融体制、国有企业等重点领域和关键环节改革加快推进。出台了一系列稳定外需的政策措施，全年进出口总额达

改善金融服务，加大金融支持经济发展的力度，积极发挥金融业在拉动内需、支持经济回升中的重要作用。金融改革稳步推进，跨境贸易人民币结算试点启动，人民币国债开始在香港公开发行，人民币国际化迈出了重要步伐。人民币汇率保持在合理均衡水平上的基本稳定，年末人民币对美元汇率中间价为 6.8282 元，升值幅度为 0.09%。

银行业保持稳健运行，风险抵御能力大幅提升

2009 年，中国银行业加大信贷投放，逆周期支持经济回升向好取得成效。国家开发银行商业化转型和农业银行股份制改革扎实推进，消费金融公司试点审批工作启动，银行入股保险公司政策开闸，全国银行业金融机构体制机制改革进一步深化。银行业实现税后利润 6624.71 亿元。商业银行不良贷款率为 1.58%，比年初下降 0.84 个百分点。商业银行资本质量维持在国际同业较高水平，普通股占比超过 80%，杠杆率在全球处于安全区间。穆迪公司将中国的主权评级展望由“稳定”调升为“正面”。银行业抗风险能力大幅提高，国际声誉显著提升。截至 2009 年年末，银行业金融机构总资产达 78.8 万亿元，增长 26.3%。

资本市场创新发展，市场体系建设迈出重要步伐

2009 年，中国资本市场总体保持安全平稳运行，功能得到较好发挥。直接融资市场加快改革步伐，新股发行工作重新启动，全年有 9 家企业在主板发行上市，90 家企业在中小板和创业板上市，150 家上市公司再融资，56 家公司并购重组，6 家企业境外上市，境内资本市场全年融资额达 4466 亿元，居历史第二高位，钢铁、汽车、煤炭等行业通过并购重组达到或正在达到产业整合、产业升级或国有经济布局调整的目标。创业板正式推出，为自主创新及成长型创业企业开辟了新的融资渠道。期货市场品种规模迅速扩大，成交总额达 130.5 万亿元，较上年增长 81.5%，对产业链相关企业服务能力明显增强。股票指数总体上行，成交量放大。上证、深证综合指数全年分别上涨 80% 和 111%，深、沪两市累计成交金额达 58.2 万亿元，较上年增长 62.4%。

保险行业平稳健康发展，与资本市场联系更加紧密

中国保险业有力应对国际金融危机，有序推动监管创新，有效促进科学发展，业务发展好于年初预期，行业风险得到有效防范，结构调整取得积极进展，市场秩序逐步好转，经营效益大幅提升，整体实力明显增强。2009 年年末，保险公司总资产达到 4.1 万亿元，净资产达到 4604.8 亿元，比上年年末增加 1441.8 亿元。保险资金运用余额为 3.7 万亿元，投资收益达 2141.7 亿元，收益率为 6.41%，比上年提高 4.5 个百分点。银行和保险公司间相互投资和开展深层次合作的瓶颈被打破，保险投资渠道不断拓宽，保险业在金融体系中的作用进一步凸显。

专栏一

应对国际金融危机的一揽子计划

2008 年 9 月，国际金融危机集中爆发并迅速席卷全球，我国经济受到严重冲击，经济社会发展形势极其严峻。党中央、国务院准确判断形势，11 月上旬及时出台进一步扩大内需、促进经济平稳较快增长的十项措施，果断实施积极的财政政策和适度宽松的货币政策，大规模增加政府投资，带动总额达 4 万亿元的两年投资计划。进入 2009 年之后，又进一步从加大财政货币政策支持、扩大内需与稳定外需结合、出台重点产业调整振兴规划、加强科技支撑和培育新兴产业、大幅度提高社会保障水平等方面，制定出台了一系列远近结合、标本兼治的政策措施，形成了应对国际金融危机、促进经济平稳较快增长的一揽子计划。

专栏二

新修订《保险法》颁布实施

2009 年 2 月 28 日，十一届全国人大常委会第七次会议通过《中华人民共和国保险法》修订草案。新修订的《保险法》于 2009 年 10 月 1 日起实施。与原法相比，新法在保险合同法律规范、保险行业基本制度、保险监管等方面进行了完善，更加注重保护被保险人利益，进一步规范了保险业务规则，加大了对违法行为的责任追究。新修订《保险法》的颁布，是我国保险业发展历史上的一件大事，是我国保险法制走向完善和成熟的重要标志，将对保险业发展产生积极而深远的影响。

专栏三

商业银行获准参股保险公司

2008 年 1 月 16 日，中国银监会与中国保监会签署《关于加强银保深层次合作和跨业监管合作谅解备忘录》，规定银行和保险公司按照市场化和平等互利原则，可以开展相互投资试点。2009 年 11 月 26 日，中国银监会正式发布《商业银行投资保险公司股权试点管理办法》，对试点机构准入条件、申请程序、风险控制及监督管理等方面提出了具体标准。开展商业银行投资保险公司股权试点工作，将有利于促进银行业和保险业资源共享、优势互补，更好地满足消费者日益增长的多元化金融服务需求。

叁

保险业服务和谐社会建设

- 促进经济平稳较快增长
- 服务『三农』发展
- 参与多层次社会保障体系建设
- 维护社会和谐稳定

2009 年，保险业深入贯彻落实科学发展观，坚持“想全局、干本行，干好本行、服务全局”，在保障经济平稳增长、促进民生改善、维护社会稳定等方面发挥了积极作用。

保险业服务和谐社会建设

促进经济平稳较快增长

贯彻落实国务院关于“稳定外需、扩大内需”的政策措施，大力发展信用保险和保证保险。2009 年，信用保险为国内外贸易承担风险金额 9114.6 亿元，同比增长 82.6%。其中，短期出口信用险累计承保额 902.7 亿美元，是 2008 年的 2.2 倍，超额完成国务院部署的 840 亿美元承保任务；大型成套设备出口融资保险完成承保方案 86 个，涉及合同金额 305 亿美元，是 2008 年的 6 倍；出口信用保险对我国一般贸易出口渗透率由 2008 年的 6.5% 提高到 18.6%。主动服务国家十大重点产业调整振兴规划，积极推动新型车贷保险、小额贷款保证保险和科技保险试点，保证保险承担风险金额达 2299.9 亿元。

服务“三农”发展

农业保险规模稳步扩大。2009 年，我国农业保险实现保费 133.9 亿元，同比增长 21%，提供风险保障 3812.1 亿元，同比增长 59%；参保农户 1.33 亿户次，同比增长 47.9%；种植业保险共承保农作物及林木 9.5 亿亩，养殖业保险承保大小牲畜 6946.2 万头（只），家禽 6.1 亿只。农业保险赔款金额累计 95.2 亿元，受益农户 1822.5 万户次。

保险责任范围不断拓展。种植业方面，将广大农户反映强烈的旱灾和病虫害纳入保险责任；养殖业方面，已基本承保所有动物疾病（疫病）、自然灾害、意外事故和政府扑杀保险责任。目前，我国农业保险承保的保险责任比发达国家更为广泛。

保险覆盖面继续拓宽。2009 年，在中央财政保费补贴支持的险种中新增了育肥猪保险和森林保险，中央政策性农业保险险种已达到 9 个。目前，全国开展的农村保险险种达 160 多个，覆盖了种植业、养殖业、农民人身、农户财产、养老等“三农”的各个方面。开办农业保险的保险公司达到 20 家，以全国性保险公司和专业保险公司组成的农业保险经营网络初步形成，农业保险已覆盖全国各地。

农村小额保险试点顺利推进。保险业将其作为发展农村保险的重要突破口，不断创新服务模式，扩大覆盖面。截至 2009 年年末，小额保险试点工作已扩展到 19 个省区，实现保费 2.3 亿元，为 871 万人提供 1364 亿元风险保障。

参与多层次社会保障体系建设

参与医疗卫生体制改革。贯彻落实《中共中央、国务院关于深化医药卫生体制改革的意见》，推动保险业参与社会医疗保障体系建设，为 1.6 亿人次提供基本医疗和补充医疗保险服务。争取相关部门支持，推动上海市个人税延型养老保险试点。

扩大健康保险服务范围。截至 2009 年年末，保险业共为 13 亿人次提供 28.5 万亿元健康风险保障，支付补偿金额 217 亿元。同时，健康保障委托管理业务规模稳步扩大，全年累计新增委托管理资金 69.6 亿元，为 1889.9 万人次提供赔付与补偿服务，补偿金额达 86.8 亿元。

扩大养老保障覆盖面。截至 2009 年年末，共为 1163 万人次提供了商业养老风险保障。企业年金业务迅速发展，为 6762.8 万人次提供了年金保险服务，较年初增长 13%。养老金公司收取企业年金受托业务缴费 263.6 亿元，较年初增长 28.3%；受托管理资产 708 亿元，投资管理资产 486.1 亿元，较年初分别增长 49.5% 和 28.8%。

维护社会和谐稳定

大力推动医疗、交通、教育以及环保等领域的责任保险发展，环境污染责任保险在 8 个省市试点，医疗责任保险在 16 个省区市的 56 个地市启动，成为中央综治办建立平安医院的重要措施，在化解医患事故纠纷、分担医疗责任风险方面发挥了积极作用。指导有关公司做好婴幼儿奶粉事件患儿医疗赔偿基金管理工作。积极应对东北地区旱灾和部分地区雪灾，做好理赔服务。与有关部委联合下发了 13 个推动相关业务发展的指导性文件，积极服务经济社会发展和人民生活。2009 年共承担各类责任风险保障金额 69.2 万亿元，支付补偿金 39 亿元，其中，分别为公众责任、产品责任、雇主责任、职业责任支付了 17.8 亿元、2.5 亿元、10.9 亿元、6.2 亿元补偿金，较好地发挥了社会管理功能。

专栏四

商业保险参与医疗保障体系建设

2009 年，《中共中央、国务院关于深化医药卫生体制改革的意见》和《医药卫生体制改革近期重点实施方案(2009—2011 年)》下发，明确了我国医药卫生体制改革的指导思想、基本原则、总体目标和主要政策措施，提出了建设覆盖城乡居民的多层次医疗保障体系，充分肯定了商业健康保险在国家医疗保障体系中的重要作用，对当前和今后一段时期保险业的发展具有重要指导意义。2009 年 5 月 27 日，《中国保险监督管理委员会关于保险业深入贯彻医改意见积极参与多层次医疗保障体系建设的意见》发布，对保险业如何贯彻新医改方案提出了明确的指导意见。

专栏五

《企业会计准则解释第 2 号》实施

2008 年 8 月 7 日，财政部印发了《企业会计准则解释第 2 号》，要求境内外上市保险公司对同一交易事项采用相同的会计政策和会计估计进行确认、计量和报告。中国保监会于 2009 年 1 月 5 日下发了《中国保险监督管理委员会关于保险业实施〈企业会计准则解释第 2 号〉有关事项的通知》，要求所有保险公司，无论是否在境内、境外上市，均执行新的统一的会计政策，在编制 2009 年年度财务报告时，对目前导致境内外会计报表差异的各项会计政策同时进行变更。这一规定的实施将对保险公司的会计、审计、内部控制、公司治理及发展战略等方面产生重大影响，有利于更加客观、公允地反映保险公司的财务状况和经营成果，进一步促进保险业结构调整和行业又好又快发展。

肆

现代监管制度不断完善

- 中国保险监督管理委员会职责
- 监管机构的组织框架
- 监管目标
- 保险监管理念更趋成熟
- 监管资源进一步优化整合
- 监管法规制度深入实施
- 非现场监管方式不断创新
- 市场行为监管切实加强
- 行业风险得到有效防范

1998年11月18日，中国保险监督管理委员会（以下简称中国保监会）成立，之后在29个省会城市相继设立直属派出机构。从2004年起，先后在6个计划单列市增设派出机构，目前，保险监管机构布局已覆盖除拉萨外的全部省会城市。截至2009年年末，全国保险监管工作人员共计2550人，其中保监会机关387人，派出机构2163人。

现代监管制度不断完善

中国保险监督管理委员会职责

主要职责

1. 拟订保险业发展的方针政策，制订行业发展战略和规划；起草保险业监管的法律、法规；制定行业内规章。

2. 审批保险公司及其分支机构、保险集团公司、保险控股公司的设立；会同有关部门审批保险资产管理公司的设立；审批境外保险机构代表处的设立；审批保险代理公司、保险经纪公司、保险公估公司等中介机构及其分支机构的设立；审批境内保险机构和非保险机构在境外设立保险机构；审批保险机构的合并、分立、变更、解散，决定接管和指定接受；参与、组织保险公司的破产、清算。

3. 审查、认定各类保险机构高级管理人员的任职资格；制定保险从业人员的基本资格标准。

4. 审批关系社会公众利益的险种、依法实行强制保险的险种和新开发的人寿保险险种等保险条款和保险费费率，对其他保险险种的条款和费率实施备案管理。

5. 依法监管保险公司的偿付能力和市场行为；负责保险保障基金的管理，监管保险保证金；根据法律和国家对保险资金的运用政策，制定有关规章制度，依法对保险公司的资金运用进行监管。

6. 对政策性保险和强制保险进行业务监管；对专属自保、相互保险等组织形式和业务活动进行监管。归口管理保险行业协会、保险学会等行业社团组织。

7. 依法对保险机构和保险从业人员的不正当竞争等违法、违规行为，以及对非保险机构经营或变相经营保险业务进行调查、处罚。

8. 依法对境内保险及非保险机构在境外设立的保险机构进行监管。

9. 制定保险行业信息化标准；建立保险风险评价、预警和监控体系，跟踪分析、监测、预测保险市场运行状况，负责统一编制全国保险业的数据、报表，并按照国家有关规定予以发布。

10. 承办国务院交办的其他事项。

监管机构的组织框架

- 主席
  - 副主席
  - 副主席
  - 副主席
  - 副主席
  - 纪委书记
  - 主席助理
  - 主席助理
- 办公厅
- 发展改革部
- 政策研究室
- 财务会计部
- 财产保险监管部
- 人身保险监管部
- 保险中介监管部
- 资金运用监管部
- 国际部
- 法规部
- 统计信息部
- 稽查局
- 人事教育部
- 监察局
- 机关党委

直属中国保监会的 35 个派出机构，根据授权履行行政管理职能，依照国家有关法律、法规和方针、政策，统一监督管理辖区内的保险市场，维护当地保险市场的合法、稳健运行，引导和促进当地保险业持续、快速、协调、健康发展。

监管目标

- 保护保单持有人利益
- 促进保险业持续、快速、协调发展
- 防范和化解风险

保险监管理念更趋成熟

秉承科学的监管理念，继续完善监管法律体系、三支柱监管框架和防范化解风险的五道防线，坚持防范化解风险不放松，坚持促进转变发展方式不动摇，坚持保护被保险人利益不懈怠，着力解决制约保险业平稳健康发展的结构性、制度性问题，不断增强监管的科学性、有效性和针对性。

监管资源进一步优化整合

完善监管机构设置，设立稽查局和培训中心，进一步理顺监管职责，加大违法违规行为的查处力度，加强监管干部的教育培训工作，提高科学监管的工作水平。开展保险公司法人机构属地监管试点，逐步改变会机关直接承担监管职能的单一格局，形成会机关指导、辖区保监局负责、上下分工协作的监管机制。

监管法规制度深入实施

以新修订《保险法》实施为契机，做好规章制度的废、改、立工作，修订颁布《保险公司管理规定》、《保险公司董事、监事和高级管理人员任职资格管理规定》、《保险公司中介业务违法行为处罚办法》等7部规章制度，不断健全保险监管和保险经营的制度体系，全面推进依法监管和依法经营。完善治理结构监管，成立保险公司治理监管委员会，推行车险“见费出单”制度，推广人身险“零现金”收付费制度，建立承保理赔信息网上查询制度。强化人身险市场规范经营的制度基础，建立新型产品信息披露、人身意外险业务经营标准、投保提示等监管制度。加强对法人机构的监管，强化资本约束，着手研究修改最低资本标准，建立风险提示和通报制度，建立保险集团内部风险隔离制度。

非现场监管方式不断创新

继续加强偿付能力监管，健全偿付能力监管机制，完善偿付能力监管标准。强化偿付能力监管的刚性约束，依法采取措施，先后推动45家公司增资扩股225亿元、10家公司发行次级债180亿元，督促不达标的公司改善偿付能力状况，减少资本消耗。稳步推进分类监管，完善分类监管办法，健全工作机制，把列为C类和D类的公司作为监管重点，采取了42项监管措施，基本实现分类监管与偿付能力监管的有机结合。切实加强监管信息化建设，初步建成信息化基础平台，基本覆盖非现场监管的主要领域。

市场行为监管切实加强

加大保险市场规范力度，开展数据真实性检查，整治银保和短期意外险业务，查处保险公司中介业务违法、违规行为，打击集资诈骗、侵占挪用保费等非法行为，深入推进打击“三假”专项工作。2009年，查处各类假冒保险机构案件32起、虚假赔案1.6万件，涉及保费金额超过1亿元，涉及赔案金额4.2亿元；向司法机关移送案件298件，移送442名涉案人员；共对976家次保险机构进行处罚，其中停止接受新业务51家次，吊销营业许可证35家，责令撤换高管人员113人；分别对机构和个人罚款4241万元和597万元。

行业风险得到有效防范

面对国际金融危机，积极采取一系列措施，完善风险防范机制，突出风险防范重点，加强监管国际合作，全面提升行业风险防范能力，有效地防范了风险跨境传递和各种新的风险，并且积极化解了历史遗留问题，维护了行业安全稳健运行。截至2009年年底，偿付能力不达标的保险公司共8家，比年初减少5家。资金运用监管不断加强，保险资产配置较好地实现了安全性、流动性和收益性的平衡。

专栏六

打击假机构、假保单和假赔案

深入开展打击假保险机构、假保单和假赔案“三假”专项工作，是2009年保监会加强保险监管、防范化解风险的一项重要举措。按照保监会的统一部署，全行业积极行动，出重拳、动真格，深入排查风险隐患，查处了一批“三假”案件，初步形成了多部门配合的执法协调机制，保险业打击“三假”专项工作取得了阶段性成效。2009年，中国保险业共查处各类假冒保险机构案件32起、虚假赔案1.6万件，涉及保费金额超过1亿元，涉及赔款金额4.2亿元。

专栏七

监管机构实施分类监管

为了增强保险监管的科学性、针对性和有效性，切实防范化解风险，2006年、2007年，保监会在人身保险和财产保险领域开始探索分类监管。在试点和总结经验的基础上，保监会制定了新的分类监管制度，决定从2009年1月1日起正式实施对产险、寿险公司及保险专业中介机构的分类监管。分类监管是以风险控制为着眼点的一项综合监管措施。保监会将在每年年初根据上一年度审计后的数据，对所有保险公司进行全面评价分类，决定对各公司采取的监管措施，再根据每季度的数据评估一次，对年度评价结果和监管措施进行相应调整。保险专业中介机构数量众多，保监局根据实际情况，对保险专业中介机构进行动态监管，实时评估风险，决定监管措施。

伍

保险市场运行状况

- 非寿险公司业务
- 寿险公司业务
- 专业再保险公司业务
- 保险中介市场业务
- 外资保险业务
- 保险资产管理

2009年，中国保险业共实现保费11137.3亿元，同比增长13.8%。保险深度3.32%①，同比提高0.07个百分点；保险密度834.4元，同比提高97.7元。赔款和给付金额达3125.5亿元，同比增长5.2%。保险公司总资产达到4.1万亿元，较年初增长21.6%。全国共有保险集团公司8家，保险公司120家，比2008年增加8家，保险资产管理公司9家。

执行《企业会计准则解释第2号》后，2009年全行业保险业务收入共计10057.4亿元，同比增长27.2%。其中非寿险公司保险业务收入达3001.2亿元，同比增长22.3%；寿险公司保险业务收入达6676.2亿元，同比增长29.3%；再保险公司保险业务收入达380亿元，同比增长33%。

保险市场运行状况

非寿险公司业务

保费保持较快增长

2009年，非寿险公司业务继续保持较快增长的势头，实现保费2992.9亿元，同比增长22.4%，增速比上年同期增加5.1个百分点。

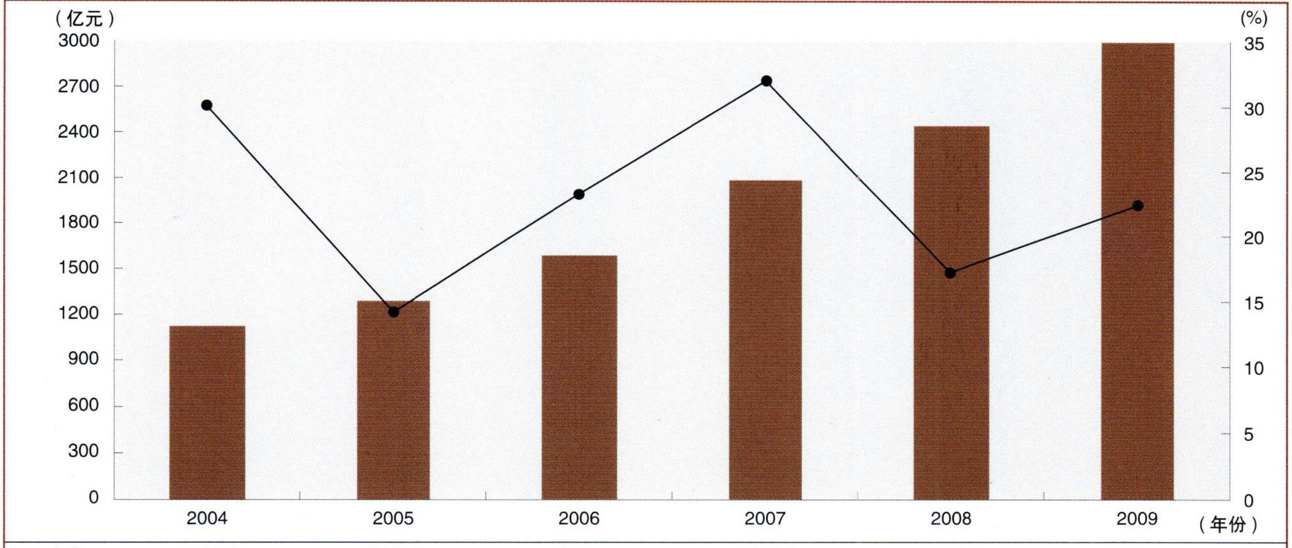

	2004	2005	2006	2007	2008	2009
保费 (左坐标)	1124.8	1283.5	1581.1	2086.6	2446.2	2992.9
增速 (右坐标)	30.0	14.1	23.2	32.0	17.3	22.4

图2　2004—2009年非寿险公司保费及增长速度

保费构成前5位的是车险、企财险、农业险、责任险和意外险，占全部保费的89.5%。

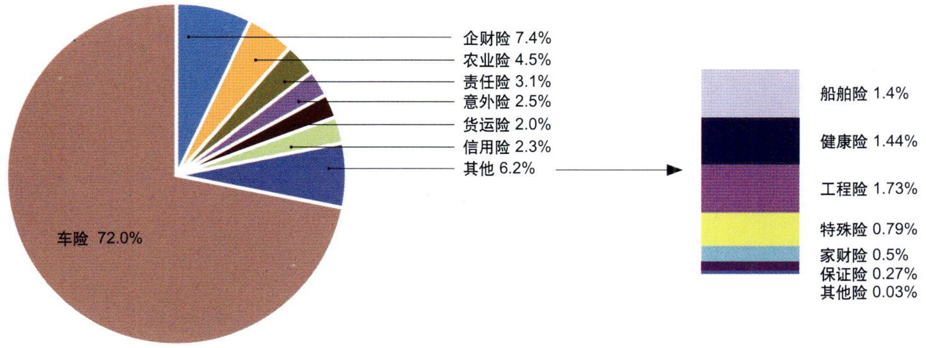

图3　2009年非寿险公司业务构成

① 保险深度和保险密度根据业务口径的保费数据计算得出。

非寿险多数险种实现稳步增长，其中车险、家财险、农业险、责任险、工程险和健康险业务分别增长 26.6%、19.1%、21%、12.8%、31.6% 和 17.1%。信用险保费增长速度达到 91.3%。

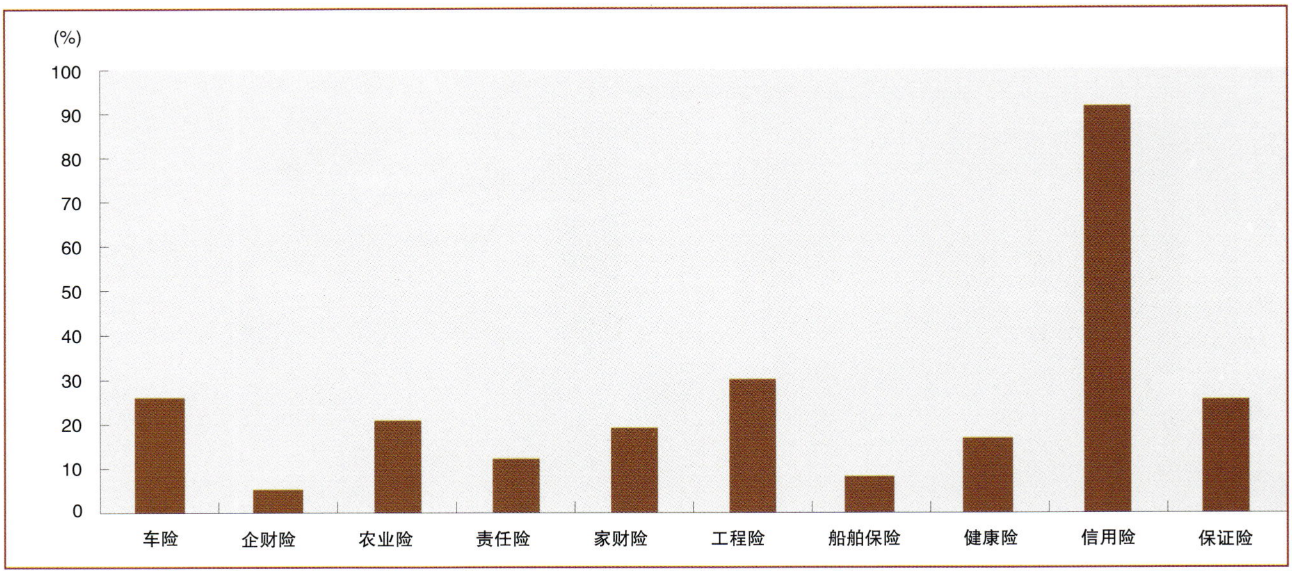

图 4　2009 年非寿险公司主要险种保费增长率

表 1　2009 年非寿险公司保费前十名

排名	名称	资本结构	保费（亿元）	市场份额（%）
1	中国人民财产保险股份有限公司	中资	1194.6	39.9
2	中国平安财产保险股份有限公司	中资	384.8	12.9
3	中国太平洋财产保险股份有限公司	中资	342.3	11.4
4	中华联合财产保险股份有限公司	中资	194.4	6.5
5	中国大地财产保险股份有限公司	中资	102.5	3.4
6	中国人寿财产保险股份有限公司	中资	79.1	2.6
7	天安保险股份有限公司	中资	70.0	2.3
8	中国出口信用保险公司	中资	68.4	2.3
9	阳光财产保险股份有限公司	中资	66.0	2.2
10	永安财产保险股份有限公司	中资	53.4	1.8
	合计		2555.5	85.3

市场主体稳步增加，市场集中度进一步降低

截至 2009 年年底，全国共有非寿险公司 52 家，其中中资公司 34 家，外资公司 18 家，全国共新增非寿险公司 5 家。非寿险市场集中度继续降低，保费前 5 家公司市场份额共计 74.1%，较上年同期减少 1.5 个百分点。

赔款金额持续增长

2009 年，非寿险公司赔款金额达 1638.2 亿元，同比增长 11.0%，增速比上年同期减少 28.1 个百分点。车险、企财险、家财险、工程险、责任险、信用险、农业险和健康险赔款金额分别比上年同期增长 14.7%、-27.6%、-20.7%、24.4%、17.7%、82.8%、48.4% 和 19.3%。2009 年，非寿险公司已赚保费综合费用率为 38.2%。

准备金余额继续上升

截至 2009 年年底，非寿险公司未到期责任准备金和未决赔款准备金达到 2430 亿元，较上年增长 18.8%。其中，非寿险公司未到期责任准备金为 1298.2 亿元，未决赔款准备金为 1131.8 亿元。

2009 年，非寿险公司提取未到期责任准备金为 232.3 亿元，提取未决赔款准备金为 151.5 亿元。

专栏八

保险公司体制改革取得重大进展

2009 年，中国保险业继续把改革作为一项基础性、战略性工作加以推进，保险公司改制上市成果进一步巩固发展。中国人民保险集团公司整体改制顺利完成，2009 年 10 月，中国人民保险集团股份有限公司正式挂牌成立。中国太平洋保险集团在香港成功上市，成为内地第四家境外上市的保险公司。中国出口信用保险公司体制改革大力推进。

专栏九

信用保险助力国家外需稳定

2009 年，为克服国际金融危机对中国外贸出口的影响，国家将完善出口信用保险政策作为稳定外需的重要政策措施。保险业积极服务经济社会发展大局，大力发展出口信用保险。2009 年，中国出口信用保险公司实现信用保险及担保金额 1166 亿美元，同比增长 85.8%。出口信用保险对我国一般贸易出口渗透率由 2008 年的 6.5% 提高到 18.6%，对稳定外贸出口发挥了重要作用。

寿险公司业务[①]

保费稳定增长

2009 年寿险公司实现保费 8144.2 亿元，占全国总保费的 73.1%，同比增长 11.0%。

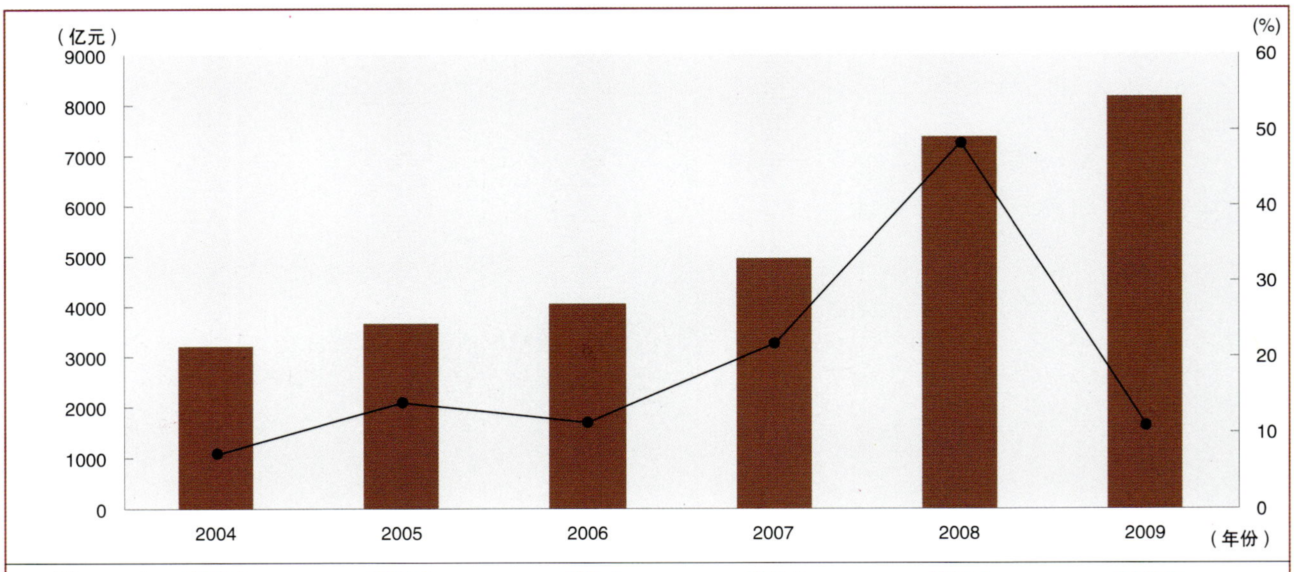

	2004	2005	2006	2007	2008	2009
保费（左坐标）	3198.2	3644.9	4059.1	4946.5	7342.6	8144.2
增速（右坐标）	7.2	14.0	11.3	21.9	48.5	11.0

图 5　2004—2009 年寿险公司保费及增长速度

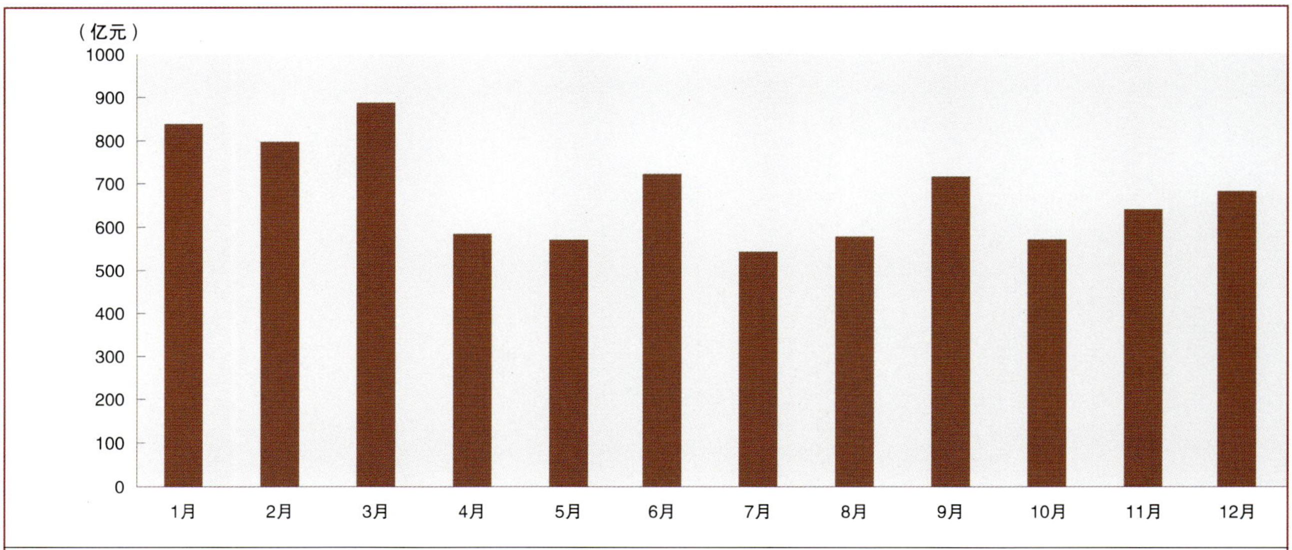

	1月	2月	3月	4月	5月	6月	7月	8月	9月	10月	11月	12月
保费	839	800	886	589	575	720	545	576	719	573	642	680

图 6　2009 年寿险公司月度保费

业务结构持续优化

截至 2009 年年底，寿险公司新单保费 5426.4 亿元，同比增长 4.8%，占寿险公司保费的 66.6%。新单标准保费 1721.4 亿元，同比增长 19.5%。新单期缴保费 1365.1 亿元，同比增长 33.4%，占寿险公司新单保费的 25.2%，占比上升了 5.4 个百分点。其中，10 年期及以上期缴保费同比增长 22.7%。

① 含专业健康保险公司和养老保险公司。

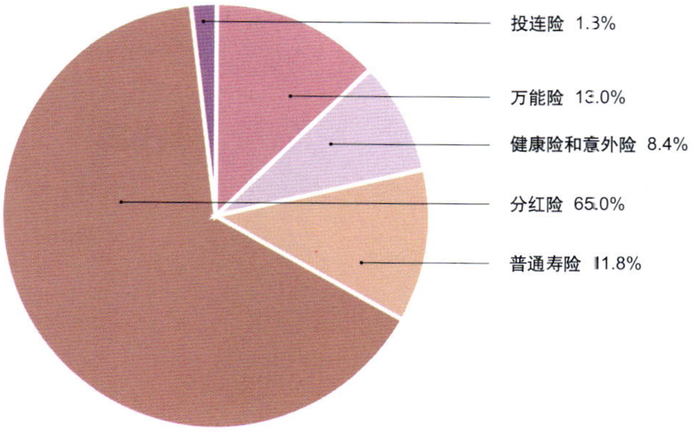

图 7　2009 年寿险公司业务构成

分红险保费快速增长

2009 年，分红险在寿险保费中的占比有较大提升，实现保费 5292.6 亿元，同比增长 39.3%，占寿险公司保费的 65%，占比较上年同期上升 13.2 个百分点，对 2009 年寿险公司保费稳定增长起到了重要作用。

万能险保费 1055.2 亿元，同比下降 27.3%，占寿险公司保费的 13%，占比下降 6.8 个百分点。投连险保费 147.9 亿元，同比下降 65.2%，占寿险公司保费的 1.8%，占比下降 4 个百分点。普通寿险保费 961.6 亿元，同比下降 2.3%，占寿险公司保费的 11.8%，占比下降 1.6 个百分点。

健康险和意外险保费合计 687 亿元，同比增长 1.1%，占寿险公司保费的 8.4%，同比下降 0.8 个百分点。

个险营销与银行邮政代理业务平稳发展

个人营销渠道实现保费 3569.3 亿元，同比增长 15.8%，占寿险公司业务总量的 43.8%。

银行邮政代理渠道实现保费 3885.9 亿元，同比增长 8.2%，占寿险公司业务总量的 47.7%。

公司直销业务实现保费 539.0 亿元，同比下降 7.8%，占寿险公司业务总量的 6.6%。

保险经纪实现保费 16.1 亿元，同比增长 12.9%。专业代理实现保费 59.2 亿元，同比增长 30.8%。

市场主体有所增加

截至 2009 年年底，全国共有人身保险公司 59 家，其中，寿险公司 50 家，专业养老保险公司 5 家，专业健康保险公司 4 家，合计增加 3 家。其中中资公司 31 家，较上年增加了百年人寿和中邮人寿 2 家，减少华泰人寿 1 家（变更为外资）；外资公司 28 家，较上年增加了汇丰人寿和华泰人寿共 2 家。

保费前 5 家公司市场份额共计 77.1%，较上年同期下降 1.5 个百分点。

表 2　2009 年寿险公司保费前十名

排名	名称	资本结构	保费（亿元）	市场份额（%）
1	中国人寿保险股份有限公司	中资	2950.4	36.2
2	中国平安人寿保险股份有限公司	中资	1323.0	16.2
3	中国太平洋人寿保险股份有限公司	中资	675.8	8.3
4	泰康人寿保险股份有限公司	中资	670.1	8.2
5	新华人寿保险股份有限公司	中资	667.8	8.2
6	中国人民人寿保险股份有限公司	中资	524.4	6.4
7	太平人寿保险有限公司	中资	225.9	2.8
8	美国友邦保险有限公司	外资	80.4	1.0
9	生命人寿保险股份有限公司	中资	70.0	0.9
10	中国人民健康保险股份有限公司	中资	62.0	0.8
	合计		7249.8	89.0

退保情况保持稳定①

2009年，寿险公司退保金为1069.7亿元，同比增长10.7%，退保率为3.54%，同比下降0.3个百分点。其中，中资寿险公司退保率为3.43%，外资寿险公司退保率为5.65%。

赔款与给付金额略有下降

寿险公司各项赔款与给付金额1487亿元，同比下降0.6%。

表3　2009年寿险公司赔款给付金额

险种	赔款给付金额（亿元）	同比增长（%）	占比（%）
寿险	1268.5	−3.5	85.3
健康险	182.8	24.7	12.3
意外险	35.7	4.7	2.4
合计	1487.0	−0.6	100.0

专业再保险公司业务

截至2009年年底，全国共有1家再保险（集团）公司，即中国再保险（集团）公司，9家专业再保险公司，即中国财产再保险股份有限公司、中国人寿再保险股份有限公司、慕尼黑再保险公司北京分公司、瑞士再保险公司北京分公司、科隆再保险公司上海分公司、劳合社再保险（中国）有限公司、法国再保险公司北京分公司、汉诺威再保险股份公司上海分公司、中国国际再保险公司北京分公司。

2009年，全国再保险公司的总分入保费为433.3亿元，同比增长4.7%；全国再保险公司的总分保赔款金额为236.3亿元，同比增长34.2%。

① 退保金及退保率为业务口径统计数据。

保险中介市场业务

2009 年，通过保险中介渠道实现的保费 9161.1 亿元①，同比增长 13.9%，占全国总保费的 82.3%。

表 4　2009 年各保险中介渠道实现保费及占比情况

销售渠道	保险代理公司	保险经纪公司	保险兼业代理机构	保险营销员	合计
保费（亿元）	328.9	244.7	4460.7	4126.9	9161.1
同比增长（%）	21.9	−0.3	7.5	22.1	13.9
保费占比（%）	3.0	2.2	40.1	37.1	82.3

专业中介机构

2009 年，全国共有保险专业中介机构 2570 家，同比增加 125 家。其中，保险代理机构 1903 家，保险经纪机构 378 家，保险公估机构 289 家。

2009 年，全国保险专业中介机构共实现经营收入 89.2 亿元，同比增长 24.9%。其中，保险专业代理机构实现佣金收入 44.8 亿元，同比增长 33.7%。保险经纪公司实现营业收入 33.1 亿元，同比增长 24.9%。保险公估公司实现业务收入 11.3 亿元，同比减少 0.96%。

兼业代理机构

截至 2009 年年底，全国共有保险兼业代理机构 148971 家，同比增长 9%。实现佣金收入 222.1 亿元，同比增长 24.6%。

表 5　2009 年保险兼业代理渠道业务结构情况

渠道名称	机构数量（家）	数量占比（%）	保费（亿元）	占比（%）	佣金收入（亿元）	佣金占比（%）
银行类	85019	57.07	3038.99	68.13	112.73	50.75
邮政类	17543	11.78	627.85	14.08	21.27	9.58
铁路	462	0.31	2.41	0.05	0.24	0.11
航空	2110	1.42	2.80	0.06	1.00	0.45
车商	18049	12.11	328.44	7.36	36.48	16.43
其他	25788	17.31	460.15	10.32	50.39	22.68
合计	148971	100.00	4460.64	100.00	222.11	100.00

保险营销员

截至 2009 年年底，全国共有保险营销员 290.6 万人，同比增长 13.5%。其中，寿险营销员 257.7 万人，同比增长 14.5%；产险营销员 32.9 万人，同比增长 6.5%。

① 本部分数据来源于保险公司和专业保险中介机构上报保险监管部门的报表。

外资保险业务

2009 年，外资保险公司实现保费 458 亿元，同比增长 17.5%，占全国保费的 4.1%，比上年提高 0.1 个百分点。各类赔款与给付金额 59.2 亿元，同比增长 40.2%。

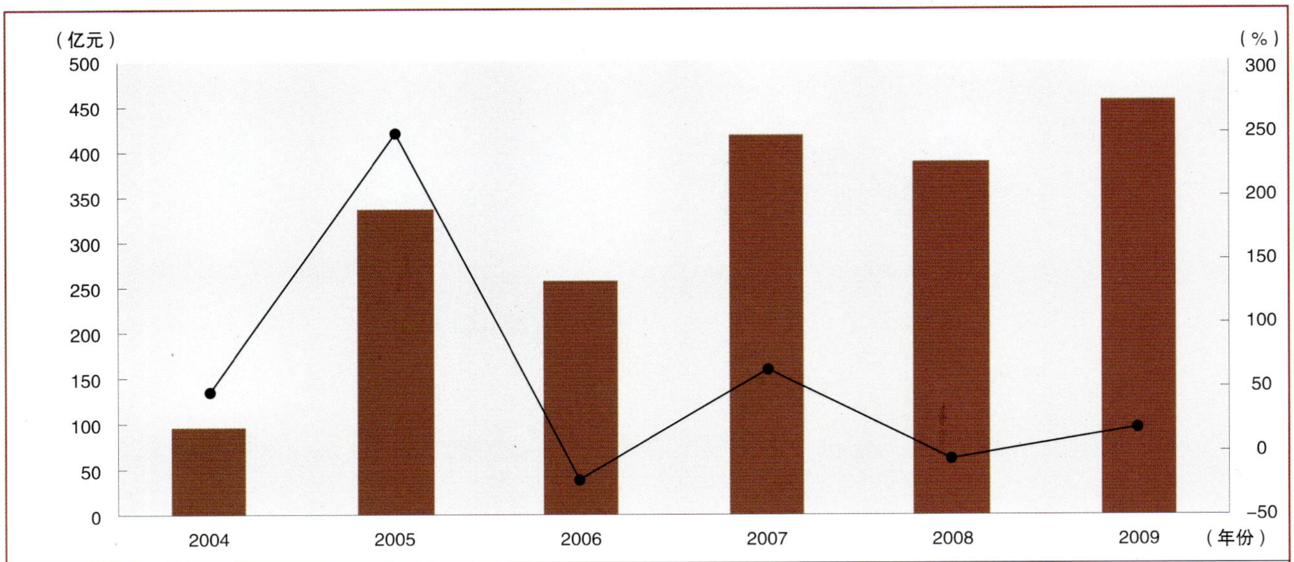

		2004	2005	2006	2007	2008	2009
保费	（左坐标）	97.9	339.3	259.4	420.5	391.2	458.0
增速	（右坐标）	45.7	246.3	−23.5	62.1	−7.0	17.5

图 8　2004—2009 年外资保险公司保费及增长率

2009 年，外资非寿险公司保费为 31.8 亿元，同比增长 10.1%，占全国非寿险公司保费的 1.1%。其中，货运险、企财险、责任险保费占外资非寿险公司业务的 74.0%。外资非寿险公司赔款金额 11.6 亿元，同比增长 24.7%；已赚保费综合费用率为 72.5%。

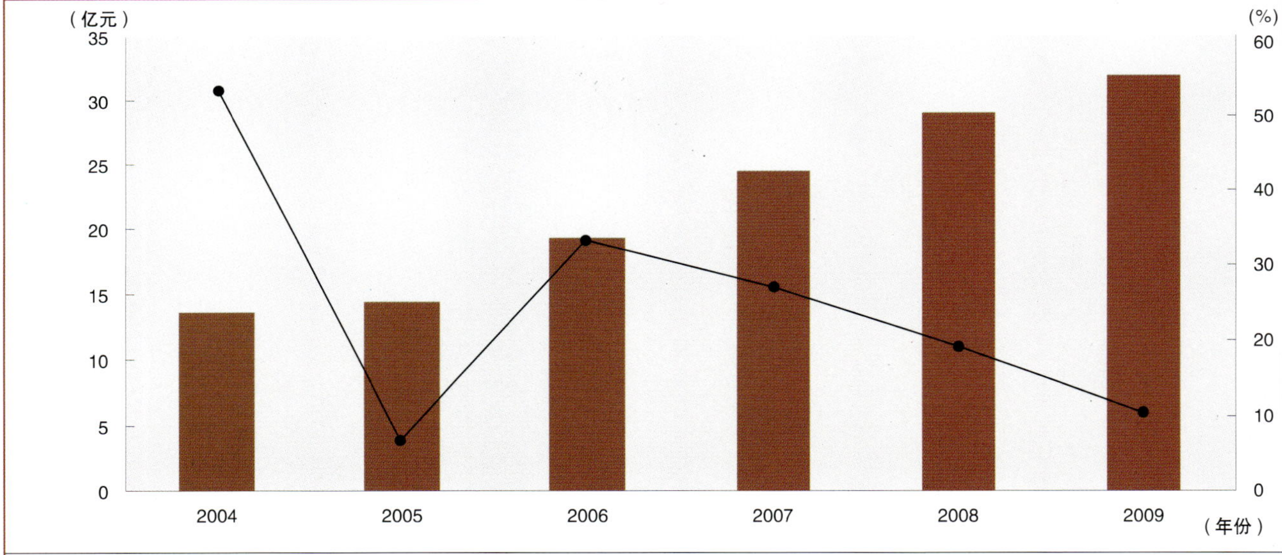

		2004	2005	2006	2007	2008	2009
保费	（左坐标）	13.6	14.5	19.2	24.3	28.9	31.8
增速	（右坐标）	52.8	6.7	32.5	26.6	18.8	10.1

图 9　2004—2009 年外资非寿险公司保费及增长率

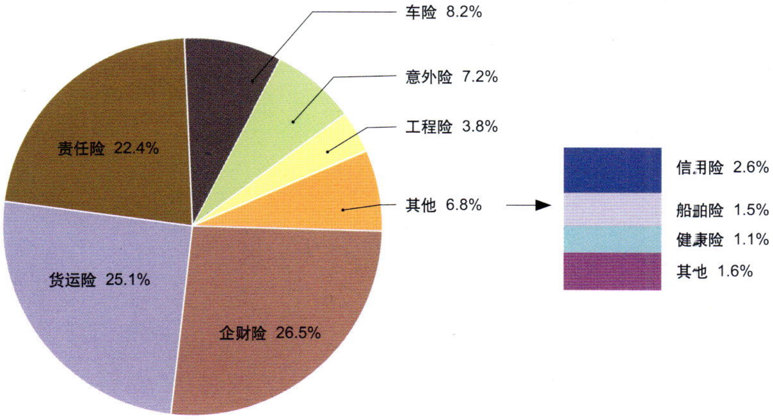

图 10　外资非寿险公司业务构成

2009 年，外资寿险公司保费为 426.3 亿元，同比增长 18.1%，占全国寿险公司保费的 5.2%。其中，新型产品（包括分红产品、投连产品和万能产品）保费 324.8 亿元，占外资寿险公司保费的 76.2%。外资寿险公司赔款给付金额为 47.3 亿元，同比增长 44.6%。退保率为 5.65%。

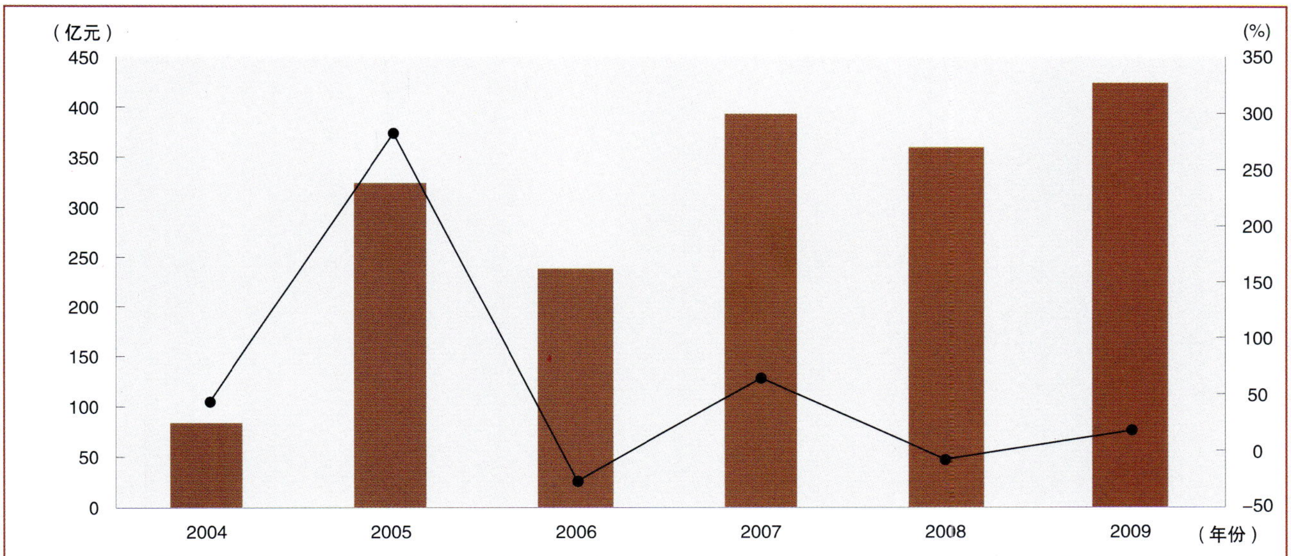

		2004	2005	2006	2007	2008	2009
保费	（左坐标）	84.4	324.8	240.2	396.2	362.3	426.3
增速	（右坐标）	44.8	284.7	−26.0	64.9	−8.6	18.1

图 11　2004—2009 年外资寿险公司保费及增长率

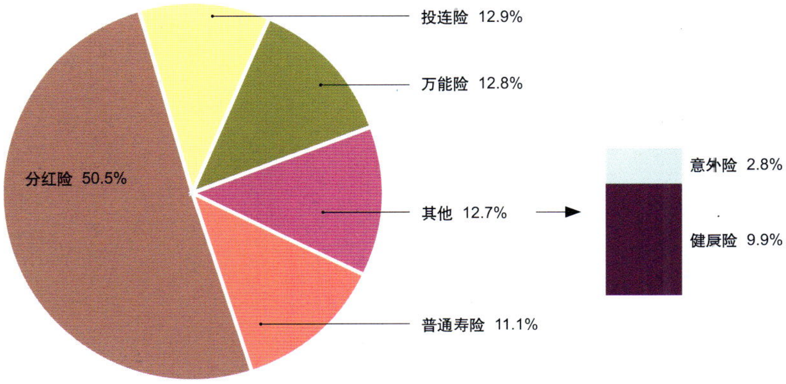

图 12　外资寿险公司业务构成

外资再保险公司分入保费为123.6亿元，同比增长81.2%，占全国再保险公司分入保费的28.5%。分保赔款金额为52.4亿元，同比增长62.7%。

截至2009年年底，全国共有52家外资保险公司，其中，非寿险公司18家，寿险公司28家，再保险公司6家，比上年新增了2家外资非寿险公司、2家外资寿险公司。

表6　外资非寿险公司市场份额前五名[①]

序号	2009年		2008年	
	名称	在外资非寿险公司中占比（%）	名称	在外资非寿险公司中占比（%）
1	美亚	25.5	美亚	29.4
2	东京海上	10.4	东京海上	14.0
3	三井住友	10.3	三井住友	10.2
4	三星	8.3	三星	9.0
5	安联	8.1	安联	7.5
	合计	62.6	合计	70.1

表7　外资寿险公司市场份额前五名

序号	2009年		2008年	
	名称	在外资寿险公司中占比（%）	名称	在外资寿险公司中占比（%）
1	友邦	18.9	友邦	20.9
2	中意	10.6	中英人寿	11.0
3	华泰人寿	10.2	信诚	10.3
4	中英人寿	9.8	中德安联	6.7
5	信诚	9.4	中意	5.8
	合计	58.9	合计	54.7

2009年，外资保险公司业务主要集中在上海、广州、深圳、北京等开放较早、发展较快的城市，上述4个城市外资保费合计占全国外资保费的63.4%，比2008年下降0.3个百分点。

表8　北京、上海、广州、深圳外资保险发展情况

城市	外资保险公司			外资非寿险公司			外资寿险公司		
	保费（亿元）	同比增长（%）	市场份额（%）	保费（亿元）	同比增长（%）	市场份额（%）	保费（亿元）	同比增长（%）	市场份额（%）
上海	112.86	13.19	24.64	13.63	−21.86	42.92	99.23	20.62	23.28
北京	100.93	35.31	22.04	4.04	52.58	12.73	96.88	34.68	22.73
广州	53.61	4.02	11.70	5.02	33.86	15.81	48.59	1.67	11.40
深圳	22.97	2.19	5.02	2.27	5.88	7.16	20.70	1.80	4.86

保险资产管理

保险行业持续发展，资金运用规模稳步增长

在政府实施积极的财政政策和适度宽松的货币政策背景下，我国宏观经济增长速度稳步回升，保险行业保费持续增

① 根据各公司保费数据计算。

长，资产规模逐步提高，资金实力进一步增强。截至 2009 年年底，保险公司总资产达到 4.1 万亿元，较 2008 年年底增长 21.6%；保险公司资金运用余额达到 37417.1 亿元，较 2008 年年底增长 22.5%。

资产配置比较稳健，保险投资取得较好收益

2009 年，受国民经济企稳向好、市场流动性充裕等因素的影响，股票市场震荡走高，上证综指年内上涨 80%。保险投资渠道稳步拓宽，投资品种范围增加。适应外部市场环境变化，保险公司调整优化资产配置，逐步降低低息长期债券的比重，减少未来利率上行导致的债券贬值风险，根据市场走势来增加权益类资产配置比例，取得了较好的投资收益。2009 年，保险公司资金运用收益共计 2141.7 亿元，资金运用平均收益率为 6.41%。

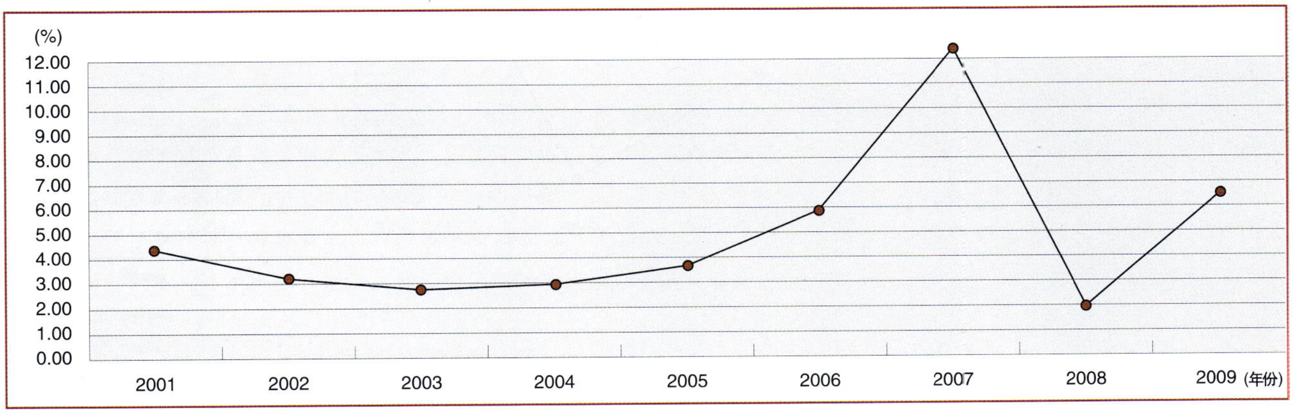

图 13　2001—2009 年保险行业资金投资收益率

保险资产管理制度不断完善，可投资品种逐步有序放开

2009 年，监管机构推出了一系列保险资产管理规范性文件，继续深入完善制度建设，细化投资管理规定，扩大资产配置空间。2009 年 3 月下发了《关于规范保险机构股票投资业务的通知》，进一步要求公司改进股票资产配置管理、加强市场风险动态监测、提高保险机构自主配置和投资管理能力。发布《关于保险资金投资基础设施债权投资计划的通知》，稳步推进保险资金投资交通、通信、能源等基础设施项目，拓宽保险机构投资渠道。发布《关于增加保险机构债券投资品种的通知》，调整债券投资政策，增加投资品种范围，改善资产配置。2009 年 8 月下发了《关于加强保险机构债券回购业务管理的通知》，要求保险公司完善债券回购管理制度、加强回购融入资金管理、防范债券回购业务风险。2009 年 12 月下发《关于保险机构投资无担保企业债券有关事宜的通知》，加强无担保债券投资管理，规范投资行为，防范投资风险。

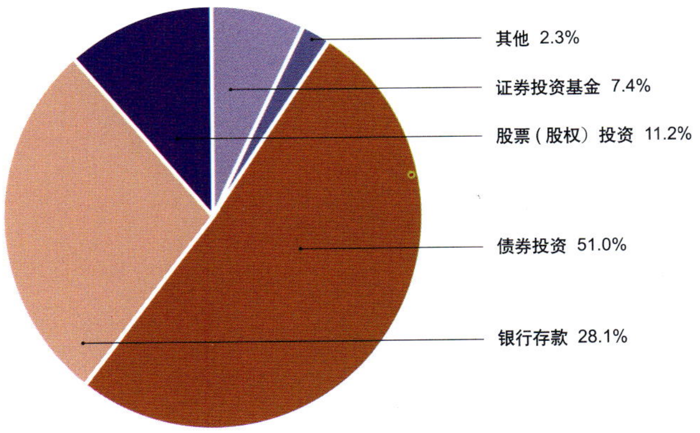

图 14　保险资金运用结构

保险资产管理风险控制取得新的进展

2009 年，监管机构加强窗口指导，积极调整投资政策，制定投资管理能力标准，进一步加强保险资产风险管控。2009 年 2 月下发了《关于加强保险资产配置风险管理的通知》，要求保险公司防范产品定价、资产错配和利率风险，加强保险资产配置风险管理，切实防范系统性风险。2009 年 3 月制定发布《保险公司股票投资管理能力标准》和《保险机构信用风险管理能力标准》，着力提升资产管理能力、控制投资风险、维护资产安全。

陆

2010年中国保险市场发展展望

- 总体向好的发展环境为保险业发展提供更多机遇
- 保险业有望在转变发展方式中保持平稳较快发展

2010年，中国经济社会将克服国际金融危机带来的不利影响和困难，继续保持较好发展势头。保险业将坚持转方式、调结构、防风险、促发展，保持行业平稳较快发展的局面。

2010年中国保险市场发展展望

总体向好的发展环境为保险业发展提供更多机遇

2010年是中国继续应对国际金融危机、保持经济平稳较快发展、加快转变经济发展方式的关键一年。中国将继续实施积极的财政政策和适度宽松的货币政策，更加注重促进发展方式转变和经济结构调整，进一步改革分配制度，城乡居民收入有望持续提高，为保险业发展提供良好的外部环境。与此同时，社会保障体系的不断完善、医疗体制改革的不断推进等，进一步巩固了保险业的发展基础，行业发展空间更为广阔。值得注意的是，虽然2010年的发展环境可能好于上年，但我国经济回升的基础还不牢固，经济发展形势仍然十分复杂，保险业发展存在较多不确定因素，对行业防范风险也提出了更高的要求。

保险业有望在转变发展方式中保持平稳较快发展

2010年，中国保险业将把转变发展方式作为重要战略任务，把稳增长建立在提高质量、优化结构、增加效益、改善服务的基础上，大力推动行业从外延式发展向内涵式发展的转变、从同质化竞争向差异化竞争转变、从粗放开发资源向和谐利用资源转变。新的一年，随着保险业不断探索和创新发展，保险市场有望继续保持平稳较快发展态势。

柒

附录

- 2009年中国保险市场重要监管动态
- 2002—2009年中国主要经济社会指标
- 2002—2009年中国主要金融指标
- 2002—2009年中国主要保险指标
- 中国重要经济金融网站

2009 年中国保险市场重要监管动态

1.《关于进一步加强投资连结保险销售管理的通知》

2009 年 1 月 23 日由保监会发布，目的是加强投连险销售管理，确保通过合格的销售人员，经由合适的销售渠道，将投连险销售给具有相应风险承受能力的客户人群，消除误导可能产生的根源，减少纠纷投诉，保护保险消费者利益。

2.《中华人民共和国保险法（修订）》

2009 年 2 月 28 日由中华人民共和国第十一届全国人民代表大会常务委员会第七次会议修订通过，自 2009 年 10 月 1 日起施行。新修订《保险法》进一步明确了对被保险人利益的保护，强化了保险监管和风险防范，拓宽了保险服务领域，对保险业依法合规经营提出了更高的要求。

3.《保险监管人员行为准则》、《保险从业人员行为准则》

2009 年 2 月 28 日由保监会发布，针对当前保险行业队伍方面存在的不足，分别对监管人员和经营从业人员的执业行为提出倡导性和禁止性的要求，这对进一步提高保险监管人员和保险从业人员整体素质、规范保险监管人员和保险从业人员职业行为具有重要意义。

4.《关于规范政策性农业保险业务管理的通知》

2009 年 4 月 13 日由保监会发布，进一步规范了政策性农业保险业务管理，对保护投保农户的合法权益、促进政策性农业保险业务平稳健康发展具有重要意义。

5.《关于保险业深入贯彻医改精神　积极参与多层次医疗保障体系建设的意见》

2009 年 5 月 27 日由保监会发布，目的是贯彻落实中共中央、国务院下发的《关于深化医药卫生体制改革的意见》和《医药卫生体制改革近期重点实施方案（2009—2011 年）》，对指导商业健康保险发展、发挥商业保险在国家医疗保障体系中的积极作用提出了重要的指导意见。

6.《关于进一步加强结构调整　转变发展方式　促进寿险业平稳健康发展的通知》

2009 年 8 月 2 日由保监会发布，从明确结构调整原则、丰富结构调整内涵、完善结构调整评价指标等方面加强指导，全方位、多层次推进寿险业结构调整。《通知》对进一步深化行业对结构调整的认识、促进寿验业平稳健康发展具有重要意义。

7.《关于防范车险理赔环节风险的通知》

2009 年 8 月 18 日由保监会发布，要求保险公司进一步加强车险理赔管理制度建设，严格管控风险、提高车险理赔服务质量，切实保护被保险人和道路交通事故受害人的合法权益。

8.《保险公司管理规定》

2009 年 9 月 25 日由保监会发布，自 2009 年 10 月 1 日起施行，《规定》对进一步改善保险监管的手段和效果、促进保险公司经营管理体制改革意义重大，有利于提高保险服务水平，更加充分地保护投保人、被保险人利益。

9.《人身保险新型产品信息披露管理办法》

2009 年 9 月 25 日由保监会发布，自 2009 年 10 月 1 日起施行，《办法》提出进一步提高信息披露的及时性、准确性和透明性，增强保险公司的强制披露义务，对于规范保险公司宣传销售行为、遏制销售误导具有重要作用。

10.《保险专业代理机构监管规定》、《保险经纪机构监管规定》、《保险公估机构监管规定》

2009 年 9 月 25 日由保监会发布，自 2009 年 10 月 1 日起施行，进一步完善了保险中介监管制度体系，有利于中介机构专业素质、管理能力、服务水平和资本实力的提升，保证保险中介行业持续、稳定、健康的发展方向。

>> 附录二

2002—2009 年中国主要经济社会指标

附表 1 2002—2009 年国内生产总值及结构

年份	国内生产总值		第一产业		第二产业		第三产业	
	绝对值（亿元）	增长率（%）	绝对值（亿元）	增长率（%）	绝对值（亿元）	增长率（%）	绝对值（亿元）	增长率（%）
2002	120333	9.1	16239	2.9	53897	9.8	50197	10.4
2003	135823	10.0	17069	2.5	62436	12.7	56318	9.5
2004	159878	10.1	20956	6.3	73904	11.1	65018	10.0
2005	182321	9.9	22718	5.2	86208	11.4	73395	9.6
2006	210871	11.1	24737	5.0	103162	13.0	82972	10.8
2007	249530	11.9	28095	3.7	121381	13.4	100054	12.6
2008	300670	9.0	34000	5.5	146183	9.3	120487	9.5
2009	335353	8.7	35477	4.2	156958	9.5	142918	8.9

注：数据来自《2009 中国统计年鉴》和 2009 年国家统计局统计公报。

附表 2 2002—2009 年年底总人口、出生率及自然增长率

年份	年底总人口（万人）	出生率（‰）	自然增长率（‰）
2002	128453	12.86	6.45
2003	129227	12.41	6.01
2004	129988	12.29	5.87
2005	130756	12.40	5.89
2006	131448	12.09	5.28
2007	132129	12.10	5.17
2008	132802	12.14	5.08
2009	133474	12.13	5.05

注：数据来自《2009 中国统计年鉴》和 2009 年国家统计局统计公报。

附表 3 2002—2009 年城镇登记失业人数及城镇登记失业率

年 份	城镇登记失业人数（万人）	城镇登记失业率（%）
2002	770	4.0
2003	800	4.3
2004	827	4.2
2005	839	4.2
2006	847	4.1
2007	830	4.0
2008	886	4.2
2009	921	4.3

注：数据来自《2009 中国统计年鉴》和 2009 年国家统计局统计公报。

附表 4　2002—2009 年农村居民家庭人均纯收入和城镇居民家庭人均可支配收入

年份	农村居民家庭人均纯收入		城镇居民家庭人均可支配收入	
	绝对值（元）	增长率（%）	绝对值（元）	增长率（%）
2002	2476	4.8	7703	13.4
2003	2622	4.3	8472	9.0
2004	2936	6.8	9422	7.7
2005	3255	6.2	10493	9.6
2006	3587	7.4	11759	10.4
2007	4140	9.5	13786	12.2
2008	4761	8.0	15781	8.4
2009	5153	8.5	17175	9.8

注：数据来自《2009 中国统计年鉴》和 2009 年国家统计局统计公报。

附表 5　2002—2009 年全社会固定资产投资总额

年 份	全社会固定资产投资总额（亿元）	增长率（%）
2002	43500	16.9
2003	55567	27.7
2004	70477	26.6
2005	88604	25.7
2006	109870	24.0
2007	137239	24.8
2008	172291	25.5
2009	224846	30.1

注：数据来自《2009 中国统计年鉴》和 2009 年国家统计局统计公报。

附表 6　2002—2009 年居民消费价格指数和固定资产投资价格指数

年 份	居民消费价格指数（上年 =100）	固定资产投资价格指数（上年 =100）
2002	99.2	100.2
2003	101.2	102.2
2004	103.9	105.6
2005	101.8	101.6
2006	101.5	101.5
2007	106.4	105.5
2008	105.9	108.9
2009	99.3	97.6

注：数据来自《2009 中国统计年鉴》和 2009 年国家统计局统计公报。

附表 7　2002—2009 年进出口总额

年份	进出口总额（亿美元）	增长率（%）
2002	6208	21.8
2003	8512	37.1
2004	11548	35.7
2005	14221	23.2
2006	17607	23.8
2007	21738	23.5
2008	25616	17.8
2009	22072	-13.9

注：数据来自国家统计局统计公报。

附表 8　2002—2009 年财政收支总额

年份	财政收入总额（亿元）	增长率（%）	财政支出总额（亿元）	增长率（%）
2002	18903.64	15.4	22053.15	16.7
2003	21715.25	14.9	24649.95	11.8
2004	26396.47	21.6	28486.89	15.6
2005	31649.29	19.9	33930.28	19.1
2006	38760.20	22.5	40422.73	19.1
2007	51321.78	32.4	49781.35	23.2
2008	61330.35	19.5	62592.66	25.7
2009	68476.88	11.7	75873.64	21.2

注：数据来自《2009 中国统计年鉴》和 2009 年国家统计局统计公报。

>> 附录三

2002—2009 年中国主要金融指标

附表 1　2002—2009 年全国城乡居民人民币储蓄存款余额

年份	全国城乡居民储蓄存款余额（亿元）	年增加额（亿元）
2002	86911	13233
2003	103617	16632
2004	119555	15929
2005	141051	21497
2006	161587	20544
2007	172534	10947
2008	217885	45351
2009	260772	42887

注：数据来自《2009 中国统计年鉴》和 2009 年国家统计局统计公报。

附表 2　2002—2009 年上市公司数量、股票发行量和股票筹资额

年份	上市公司数量（个）	股票发行量（亿股）	股票筹资额（亿元）
2002	1224	291.74	961.75
2003	1287	281.43	1357.75
2004	1377	227.92	1510.94
2005	1381	567.05	1882.51
2006	1434	1287.77	5594.29
2007	1550	637.24	8680.17
2008	1625	180.29	3852.21
2009	1718	—	—

注：数据来自《2009 中国统计年鉴》和 2009 年国家统计局统计公报。

附表 3　2002—2009 年黄金储备、外汇储备

年 份	黄金储备（万盎司）	外汇储备（亿美元）
2002	1929	2864.07
2003	1929	4032.51
2004	1929	6099.32
2005	1929	8188.72
2006	1929	10663.40
2007	1929	15282.49
2008	1929	19460.30
2009	3389	23991.52

注：数据来自《2009 中国统计年鉴》和中国人民银行网站（www.pbc.gov.cn）。

附表 4　2002—2009 年汇率

年 份	一美元折合人民币（期末数）	一美元折合人民币（平均数）
2002	8.2773	8.2769
2003	8.2767	8.2770
2004	8.2765	8.2768
2005	8.0702	8.1949
2006	7.8087	7.9735
2007	7.3046	7.3676
2008	6.8346	6.8424
2009	6.8282	6.8279

注：数据来自中国人民银行网站（www.pbc.gov.cn）。

2002—2009 年中国主要保险指标

附表 1　2002—2009 年保费及结构

年份	保费		寿险公司		非寿险公司	
	绝对值（亿元）	增长率（%）	绝对值（亿元）	增长率（%）	绝对值（亿元）	增长率（%）
2002	3048.3	44.1	2275.1	59.7	773.2	11.9
2003	3848.8	26.3	2983.2	31.1	865.6	12.0
2004	4323.0	12.3	3198.2	7.2	1124.8	30.0
2005	4928.4	14.0	3644.9	14.0	1283.1	14.1
2006	5640.2	14.4	4059.1	11.3	1581.1	23.2
2007	7033.4	25.0	4946.5	21.9	2086.6	32.0
2008	9789.1	39.2	7342.6	48.5	2446.2	17.3
2009	11137.3	13.8	8144.2	11.0	2992.9	22.4

附表 2　2009 年各地区保费情况

地区	保费			财产保险			人身保险		
	本年累计(万元)	同比增长(%)	占比(%)	本年累计(万元)	同比增长(%)	占比(%)	本年累计(万元)	同比增长(%)	占比(%)
全国合计	111372989.22	13.83	100.00	28758335.46	23.09	100.00	82614653.76	10.93	100.00
一、集团、总公司本级	251913.64	68.09	0.23	244835.44	99.06	0.85	7078.20	−69.81	0.01
二、东部地区	65178625.17	13.36	58.52	17339672.08	20.81	60.29	47838953.09	10.88	57.91
北京	6975952.11	19.05	6.26	1644197.29	22.57	5.72	5331754.82	18.01	6.45
天津	1512872.70	−13.86	1.36	457959.19	9.51	1.59	1054913.51	−21.16	1.28
河北	6010863.64	25.07	5.40	1286741.63	24.75	4.47	4724122.01	25.15	5.72
辽宁	3454932.62	5.10	3.10	864687.09	27.28	3.01	2590245.53	−0.68	3.14
大连	1163310.58	8.28	1.04	328789.23	20.46	1.14	834521.35	4.14	1.01
上海	6650258.77	10.83	5.97	1518069.76	15.19	5.28	5132189.01	9.60	6.21
江苏	9077307.31	17.06	8.15	2283865.88	26.10	7.94	6793441.43	14.31	8.22
浙江	5380952.46	9.98	4.83	1963373.42	20.42	6.83	3417579.04	4.77	4.14
宁波	1074435.32	23.35	0.96	510768.02	26.61	1.78	563667.30	20.53	0.68
福建	2722579.82	11.67	2.44	726691.12	17.85	2.53	1995888.70	9.58	2.42
厦门	583933.42	24.57	0.52	194160.09	24.43	0.68	389773.33	24.65	0.47
山东	6775768.68	18.61	6.08	1736748.71	27.78	6.04	5039019.98	15.75	6.10
青岛	1153100.85	12.25	1.04	343380.04	21.27	1.19	809720.81	8.82	0.98
广东	9595713.73	8.53	8.62	2391023.09	15.08	8.31	7204690.65	6.52	8.72
深圳	2715944.75	12.78	2.44	970684.25	14.41	3.38	1745260.50	11.89	2.11
海南	330698.40	9.99	0.30	118533.28	12.96	0.41	212165.13	8.40	0.26
三、中部地区	25830975.09	12.92	23.19	5377037.52	24.43	18.70	20453937.57	10.24	24.76

续表

地区	保费			财产保险			人身保险		
	本年累计(万元)	同比增长(%)	占比(%)	本年累计(万元)	同比增长(%)	占比(%)	本年累计(万元)	同比增长(%)	占比(%)
山西	2892494.53	10.87	2.60	671258.36	11.70	2.33	2221236.17	10.62	2.69
吉林	1848668.86	16.33	1.66	404585.90	25.55	1.41	1444082.96	13.98	1.75
黑龙江	2783743.02	10.82	2.50	567223.28	18.29	1.97	2216519.74	9.06	2.68
安徽	3572103.89	20.46	3.21	875885.04	36.95	3.05	2696218.85	15.93	3.26
江西	1871351.38	9.21	1.68	441298.59	31.90	1.53	1430052.79	3.70	1.73
河南	5653913.96	8.95	5.08	977354.13	25.54	3.40	4676559.83	6.03	5.66
湖北	3724234.43	17.43	3.34	689729.65	25.43	2.40	3034504.78	15.75	3.67
湖南	3484465.02	11.51	3.13	749702.58	21.67	2.61	2734762.45	9.01	3.31
四、西部地区	20111475.30	16.12	18.06	5796790.41	26.93	20.16	14314684.89	12.25	17.33
重庆	2447045.41	22.02	2.20	470583.98	24.64	1.64	1976461.43	21.41	2.39
四川	5790282.92	17.15	5.20	1487178.89	35.50	5.17	4303104.03	11.91	5.21
贵州	952286.64	19.10	0.86	360529.34	26.14	1.25	591757.30	15.19	0.72
云南	1800824.56	8.88	1.62	681665.27	23.48	2.37	1119159.29	1.57	1.35
西藏	40141.73	23.48	0.04	34250.11	19.60	0.12	5891.62	52.25	0.01
陕西	2595947.64	19.20	2.33	605288.30	30.82	2.10	1990659.35	16.07	2.41
甘肃	1143842.26	17.38	1.03	270537.53	19.63	0.94	873304.73	16.70	1.06
青海	182081.85	29.08	0.16	79624.38	26.85	0.28	102457.47	30.87	0.12
宁夏	392775.13	23.55	0.35	118414.47	24.97	0.41	274360.66	22.95	0.33
新疆	1566941.66	2.74	1.41	518242.23	17.11	1.80	1048699.42	-3.13	1.27
内蒙古	1713104.21	21.20	1.54	673405.08	25.65	2.34	1039699.12	18.48	1.26
广西	1486201.29	11.34	1.33	497070.82	24.13	1.73	989130.47	5.86	1.20

注：表中各地区保费及全国合计值均为业务统计数据。

附表 3　2002—2009 年保险深度、保险密度

年份	保险深度（%）	保险密度（元 / 人）
2002	2.98	237.64
2003	3.33	287.44
2004	3.39	332.16
2005	2.70	375.64
2006	2.80	431.30
2007	2.93	532.42
2008	3.25	736.74
2009	3.32	834.41

附表 4　2002—2009 年保险资金运用收益率

年份	资金运用收益率（%）
2002	3.14
2003	2.68
2004	2.87
2005	3.60
2006	5.80
2007	12.17
2008	1.91
2009	6.41

附表 5　2009 年保险资产管理公司列表

排名	名称
1	中国人保资产管理股份有限公司
2	中国人寿资产管理有限公司
3	中再资产管理股份有限公司
4	平安资产管理有限责任公司
5	华泰资产管理有限公司
6	泰康资产管理有限责任公司
7	新华资产管理股份有限公司
8	太平洋资产管理有限责任公司
9	太平资产管理有限公司

附表 6　2009 年保险经纪公司经纪收入前十名

排名	名称	业务收入（万元）	市场份额（%）
1	长安保险经纪有限公司	40774.66	12.32
2	北京联合保险经纪有限公司	24999.49	7.55
3	中怡保险经纪有限责任公司	18080.71	5.46
4	江泰保险经纪有限公司	17765.79	5.37
5	韦莱保险经纪有限公司	15765.96	4.76
6	达信（北京）保险经纪有限公司	13553.44	4.09
7	竞盛保险经纪有限公司	10648.96	3.22
8	华泰保险经纪有限公司	8998.31	2.72
9	航联保险经纪有限公司	8065.86	2.44
10	长城保险经纪有限公司	7931.44	2.40

附表 7　2009 年保险代理公司代理收入前十名

排名	名称	业务收入（万元）	市场份额（%）
1	湖南邮政保险代理有限公司	14306.00	3.19
2	广州市泛华益安保险代理有限公司	9989.11	2.23
3	东莞市南枫佳誉保险代理有限公司	9148.14	2.04
4	广东南枫保险代理有限公司	9127.86	2.04
5	河北盛安保险代理有限公司	8824.13	1.97
6	四川泛华保险代理有限公司	7039.52	1.57
7	山东华康保险代理有限公司	6418.18	1.43
8	广州辉信保险代理有限公司	6117.19	1.36
9	湖北华康保险代理有限公司	5662.94	1.26
10	江苏华康保险代理有限公司	5480.96	1.22

附表 8　2009 年保险公估机构营业收入前十名

排名	名称	业务收入（万元）	市场份额（%）
1	深圳民太安保险公估股份有限公司	19719.26	17.44
2	泛华保险公估有限公司	9052.64	8.00
3	深圳市智信达保险公估有限公司	3666.29	3.24
4	上海泛华天衡保险公估有限公司	3658.37	3.23
5	深圳市联胜保险公估有限公司	3645.28	3.22
6	广州天信保险公估有限公司	3613.23	3.19
7	上海恒量保险公估有限公司	3377.96	2.99
8	广东衡量行保险公估有限公司	3213.11	2.84
9	竞胜保险公估有限公司	2947.92	2.61
10	罗便士保险公估（中国）有限公司	2915.88	2.58

>> 附录五

中国重要经济金融网站

中国人民银行http://www.pbc.gov.cn
中国银监会http://www.cbrc.gov.cn
中国证监会http://www.csrc.gov.cn
中国保监会http://www.circ.gov.cn

国家发展和改革委员会http://www.ndrc.gov.cn
财政部http://www.mof.gov.cn
人力资源和社会保障部http://www.mohrss.gov.cn
国家统计局http://www.stats.gov.cn

ANNUAL REPORT OF CHINA INSURANCE MARKET 2009

2009 中 国 保 险 市 场 年 报

01

Chairman's Address

2009 was the toughest year for China's economy since 2000 as well as a year during which the insurance industry met challenges from the global financial crisis. Facing an extremely complicated economic environment both at home and abroad, the insurance industry thoroughly applied the scientific outlook on development and earnestly implemented the requirements imposed by the Communist Party of China (CPC) Central Committee and State Council by vigorously preventing risks, further deepening reforms, accelerating the transformation of the development mode, adjusting business structures and expanding insurance service coverage. The efforts were intended to serve the overall economic and social development and they yielded remarkable results.

Better-than-expected Insurance Business Development

In 2009, National insurance premium exceeded RMB 1.00 trillion for the first time reaching RMB 1113.73 billion (+13.8% growth year-on-year (YoY))[①]. The property and casualty insurance business continued to develop fast and the premium totaled RMB 287.58 billion[②] (+23.1% YoY). The life insurance premium reached RMB 826.15 billion (+10.9% YoY). The full-year compensation pay-outs stood at RMB 312.55 billion. The economic benefits surged significantly, and the insurance companies posted a total profit of RMB 84.5 billion. Property insurance companies got out of the red and achieved a profit of RMB 7.24 billion. Life insurance companies gained a profit of RMB 70.8 billion and the business value improved markedly. The reinsurance business achieved better underwriting results. The whole industry registered an investment return of RMB 214.17 billion, with a ROI of 6.41% (+4.5% YoY). The insurance industry boasted visibly improved capabilities. As of the end of 2009, the total assets of insurance companies reached RMB 4.10 trillion, with net assets totaling RMB 460.48 billion, up RMB 144.18 billion YoY. The insurance fund application balance stood at RMB 3.7 trillion.

Effective Prevention of Industrial Risks

In 2009, the insurance industry took risk prevention as its primary task and actively adopted measures to lower the impact of the financial crisis. It implemented dynamic monitoring and stress tests to better manage industrial risk conditions, and it formulated risk emergency response plans, eliminated potential risks of insurance companies, and kept improving risk prevention mechanisms. Forty-five insurance companies were

① Unless otherwise specified, all the financial data contained in this report were audited in accordance with the *No.2 Interpretation of Accounting Standards for Business Enterprises*. Both the insurance premium and compensation pay-outs were the data based on the business statistical approach.

② The financial data in this report were offered on the basis of comparison between data of the same statistical approach, and the financial data in 2008 were traced and adjusted in line with the accounting policies after the change.

approved for an increase of RMB 22.5 billion in capital and ten companies were issued RMB 18 billion of subordinated debt to improve their solvency. Insurance companies were urged to withdraw cash reserves in full, put the settlement rate of universal insurance and the bonus distribution of participating insurance at a long-term sustainable level, and to prevent and control risks involved in discharge of new-type insurance products. Efforts were also made to develop and adjust insurance fund management systems, expand room for asset allocation and prevent mismatching risks that may have resulted from low interest rates. By the end of 2009, there were eight insurance companies that couldn't meet the solvency standards, however key solvency indicators of the unqualified companies did overall improve. The surrender rate of life insurance companies was 3.54% and the conditions were generally stable. Insurance companies enjoyed abundant cash flow. Insurance assets allocation basically achieved a balance of security, liquidity and profitability. Cross-border transmission of risks was controlled effectively.

Positive Progress Made in Structural Adjustment

In 2009, the insurance industry continued to combine structural adjustment with its practice of meeting the financial crisis and transforming the mode of development to enhance the industrial capabilities for sustainable development. With respect to property and casualty insurance, the premiums of non-vehicle insurance businesses including agricultural insurance, credit insurance and engineering insurance rose by 21%, 91.3% and 31.6% YoY respectively. The investment balance of non-life insurance investment-oriented products stood at RMB 50.64 billion, which is RMB 42.65 billion lower than that of the end of 2008. With respect to life insurance, the standard premium rose by 19.5% YoY and the growth pace was 8.6% higher than that of the actual premium. Among the new insurance policy businesses, regular premium comprised 25.2% (+5.4% YoY), and the proportion of ten-year-or-above premiums climbed by 1.7%. Individual agent services made up 43.8% (+1.8% YoY); Agency services offered by banks and post offices accounted for 47.7% (-1.2% YoY). With respect to insurance investment, the asset allocation structure kept improving showing better investment management skills.

Enhanced Capabilities of Serving Overall Social and Economic Development

In 2009, the insurance industry strived to make greater contributions to the State's goal "to guarantee economic growth, value people's livelihood and ensure social stability" and to give full play to its role as an "economic propeller". It vigorously developed export credit insurance and the short-term export credit insurance value reached USD$90.27 billion on a cumulative basis (+122.6% YoY). It also helped to solve the problems related to agriculture, farmers and rural areas, participated in the construction of a social security system and energetically developed agricultural insurance. As a result, the premium reached RMB 13.39 billion offering RMB 381.2 billion in risk coverage (+59% YoY). Rural households covered by the insurance amounted to 133 million households (+48% YoY). Pilot projects of micro insurance were carried out steadily, and the premium totaled RMB 230 million, offering 8.71 million people risk coverage in the amount of RMB 136.4 billion. Great efforts were made to give full play to insurance's role in social risk management and to push for the development of liability insurance in such fields as healthcare, transportation, education and environmental protection. The environmental pollution liability insurance has been tried in eight provinces and municipalities. Medical liability insurance has been initiated in 56 cities of 16 provinces, municipalities and autonomous regions and it serves as an important measure of the Central Committee for Comprehensive Management of Public Security for building safe hospitals. It also plays an important role in settling doctor-patient disputes and sharing medical liability risks. Positive efforts were also made in guiding relevant companies to effectively manage their medical compensation funds for babies sickened by contaminated milk powder and in settling claims related to the drought in Northeast China and snow disaster in other regions. Such efforts were made with a view to better serve the socioeconomic development and people's lives.

Outstanding Achievements in Insurance Regulatory Work

Confronted with the extremely complicated economic situations both at home and abroad in 2009, China's insurance regulatory institutions adhered to the guideline of "preventing risks, adjusting structures and stabilizing growth", and worked to achieve the fast and sound development of the whole industry. Earnest efforts were made to weather the global financial crisis which not only effectively prevented a variety of potential risks, but also helped resolve problems left over by history, improve the long-acting mechanism for risk prevention and accumulated precious experiences in weathering complicated situations. By seizing the opportunity of implementing the newly-revised *Insurance Law*, the regulators strived to improve the insurance regulatory systems and drive forward the regulation according to law in a comprehensive way. They placed emphasis on the regulation of corporate entities and enhanced regulatory effectiveness by implementing categorized regulation, intensifying solvency regulation and improving corporate governance regulation. Vigorous efforts were also made to beef up market surveillance, which brought about better market orders and a year-on-year 2.3% decline in the cancellation rate of property and casualty insurance premiums (5%). The ratio of premiums received was 3.1% (-2.9% YoY). Insurance companies boasted further improved services and financial data authenticity. Life insurance companies gradually regulated their sales practices and misguiding sales were contained to a certain extent. There were 5150 cases of insurance complaints handled in an effort to protect the insured's interest.

Despite the complicated situations in 2009, the insurance industry attained the most outstanding achievements in several years which also represented the fruits of the insurance reform since the 16th Congress of the Chinese Communist Party. I would like to take this opportunity, to express my sincere thanks on behalf of the China Insurance Regulatory Commission to all the cadre of workers inside the insurance industry, the people from all circles of life and the friends both at home and abroad who have always cared for and supported the reform and development of the Chinese insurance industry!

2010 is the last year of the 11th Five-year Plan period as well as a year that is key to the insurance industry's efforts to combat the financial crisis. The whole industry will further implement the scientific outlook on development, follow the spirit of the Central Economic Work Conference and adhere to the guideline of shifting mode of growth, adjusting structures, reducing risks and promoting development. While highlighting the transformation of the economic development mode and risk prevention, the industry will pay greater attention to improving its development foundation, service abilities, and its offer to protect the insured's interests; all with a view to promoting its fast and steady development and making greater contributions to both social and economic development.

Wu Dingfu
Chairman, China Insurance Regulatory Commission
August 30, 2010

02

Progress and Development of Economy and Society

- New Advances in China's Economy and Society Helped Expand Development Space for Insurance Industry
- Further Improved Overall National Strength of China Helped Consolidate the Foundation of the Insurance Market
- Continued Fast and Sound Growth of the Financial Industry Helped Enhance the Economic Development Capacity

2009 was the toughest year for China's economy since 2000. Under the strong leadership of the Communist Party of China (CPC) Central Committee and State Council, the Chinese people responded calmly to the impact of the global financial crisis and took the lead in bringing about an early recovery in the economy, which is another significant achievement made in China's reform and opening-up and socialist modernization drive.

Progress and Development of Economy and Society

New Advances in China's Economy and Society Helped Expand Development Space for Insurance Industry

Successfully Weathering the Global Financial Crisis

The global financial crisis spread further in 2009. The Chinese government made well-timed adjustments to its macroeconomic policies, implemented proactive fiscal policies and moderately loosened monetary policies. In particular, China launched a stimulus package aimed to boost domestic demand, revitalize industries, develop science and technologies and improve social security. The public investment by the central budget totaled RMB 924.3 billion, increased by RMB 503.8 billion YoY and was mainly targeted at low-income housing, rural livelihood projects, social undertakings, independent innovation, structural upgrading, energy conservation & discharge reduction, ecological construction, major infrastructure and post-disaster reconstruction. Total investment in fixed assets rose by 30.1% effectively filling the gap arising from declining export demand. China quickly pulled its economy out of the slump and took the lead to achieve a rebound. This made the Chinese people more confident and proud and raised China's profile in the international community.

Intensified Construction of the New Socialist Countryside

The policies aimed at benefiting farmers were further intensified centering on stabilizing grain production, increasing farmers' income, strengthening their foundation and valuing livelihoods. In 2009, the central government spent RMB 725.3 billion on the issues related to agriculture, farmers and rural areas, a rise of RMB 129.8 billion (+21.8% YoY). The minimum grains purchase price increased significantly. The plan to undertake an increased production capacity of one hundred billion jin (50 billion kilograms) of grain was launched. Rural areas saw better access to public facilities including water, electricity, gas and roads and public services such as education, medical care and social security as well as new breakthroughs in system innovation. Grain production has registered increases for six years in a row. The employment of rural workers quickly recovered. Rural per capita net income exceeded RMB 5,000 for the first time. The agricultural society developed steadily and is harmoniously paving the way for the expansion of domestic demand and development of the economy.

Great Advances in Livelihood Construction

Facing the challenges imposed by the global financial crisis, China attached great importance to people oriented policy and put the people's livelihoods first and made comprehensive arrangements while highlighting key aspects. It implemented more proactive employment policies, significantly increased education spending and energetically carried out medical and health system reforms to effectively solve the most direct and practical problems that people are most concerned with. In 2009, the central government spent RMB 42.6 billion, RMB 198.1 billion and RMB 127.7 billion on employment, education and medical care, up 59%, 23.6% and 49.5% YoY respectively.

Accelerated Improvement of the Social Security System

The pilot programs of rural pension insurance were carried out in 320 counties marking a historic stride forward in China's social security system construction. Unified basic pension insurance systems for urban workers at the provincial level were generally established. Measures concerning the transfer and renewal of pension and medical insurance relationships were released in succession. Enterprise retirees basic pension increased for the fifth consecutive year. The urban workers and residents covered by basic medical insurance numbered 401 million, and rural residents covered by the new rural cooperative medical system numbered 830 million. In 2009, the central government spent RMB 290.6 billion on social security and employment (+16.6% YoY). The national social security funds reached RMB 692.7 billion on a cumulative basis (+44.2% YoY).

Further Improved Overall National Strength of China Helped Consolidate the Foundation of the Insurance Market

An Upward Trend in China's General National Economic Situation

In 2009, China's GDP reached RMB 33.5 trillion (+8.7% YoY). The national fiscal revenue totaled RMB 6.85 trillion (+11.7% YoY), and the national foreign exchange reserve amounted to USD2.4 trillion.

Continued Promotion of Reform and Opening-up

China made further reform and opening-up a vital force that helped to tackle the financial crisis and worked to remove institutional barriers and improve the degree of opening China to the outside world. Local governments implemented the organizational reforms in an orderly manner and public institutions carried out the pilot classified reforms steadily. Reforms in resource product prices, financial and taxation systems, state-owned enterprises and other key fields and crucial sectors were advanced in an accelerated pace. A series of policies intended to stabilize export demand were formulated. The total trade value of imports and exports amounted to USD2.2 trillion. Actual utilized foreign direct investment amounted to USD90 billion. More and more Chinese companies tended to go global despite the economic downturn and their shares in the global markets remain stable.

Further Improvement of the People's Living Standard

2009 was a year in which the Chinese people enjoyed the most significantly improved livelihood and gained the most practical benefits. A series of effective measures aimed at expanding residential consumption were implemented, including providing subsidies for rural residents to purchase home appliances and motor vehicles (including motorbikes), halving the purchase tax on low-emission automobiles, reducing or exempting taxes on buying and selling homes and supporting the purchase of self-use houses. The per capita disposable income of urban residents and per capita net income of rural residents respectively registered an actual growth of 9.8% and 8.5% respectively. The full-year consumer price fell by 0.7% YoY, and a total of 11.02 million job opportunities were created for urban residents. Total retail sales of consumer goods went up by 16.9% YoY, the highest growth rate since 1986.

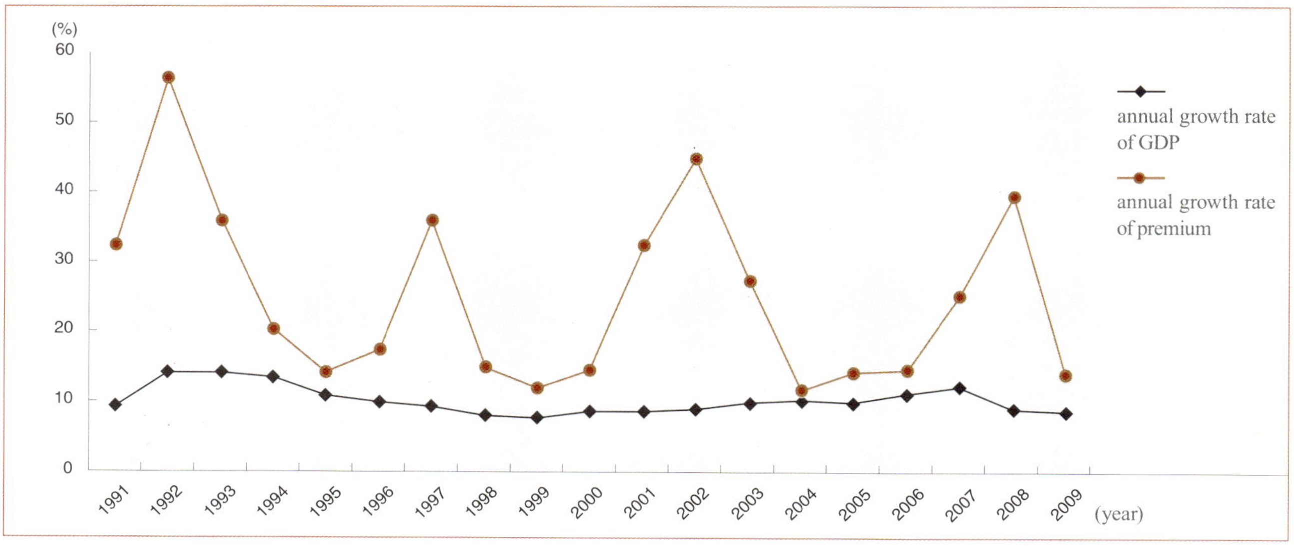

Figure 1 Comparison between GDP Growth and Annual Premium Growth from 1991 to 2009

Continued Fast and Sound Growth of the Financial Industry Helped Enhance the Economic Development Capacity

In 2009, China's financial industry stood the test of the global financial crisis and maintained its good momentum of healthy growth. The financial reform kept deepening and regulation systems kept improving. The anti-risk capability and international competitiveness of China's financial industry noticeably improved.

Moderately Loosened Monetary Policies Promoted Steady Economic Growth

In 2009, tackling the financial crisis and maintaining fast and sound economic development was regarded by the People's Bank of China as its primary task in financial regulation. To that end, the central bank implemented moderately loose monetary policies, guided financial institutions in expanding credit supply and optimized credit structure, and strived to maintain financial safety and stability. As a result, the financial industry achieved steady development. Meanwhile, effort was made to improve financial services in an all-round way, beef up the financial support for economic development and give full play to the role of financial industry in boosting domestic demand and bringing about an economic recovery. The financial reform was advanced steadily, pilot programs of RMB settlement in cross-border trade were initiated, and RMB treasury bonds were issued publicly in Hong Kong marking a big step forward for RMB internationalization. The RMB exchange rate was basically kept at a reasonable and balanced level, and the central parity of RMB against US dollar stood at RMB 6.8282 (+0.09% YoY) at the end of 2009.

Banking Industry Remained Stable with Increasingly Stronger Risk Resistance Capability

In 2009, China's banking industry increased credit supply to help the economy to recover from the recession. The commercial transformation of China Development Bank Corporation and the reform of the Agricultural Bank of China towards a joint-stock enterprise were advanced steadily. The approval work for pilot launch of consumer finance companies was initiated. Policies regarding banks' investment in insurance companies were loosened and the reforms in banking financial institutions were further deepened. The banking industry posted a post-tax profit of RMB 662.471 billion. Commercial banks registered a non-performing loans ratio of 1.58%, down 0.84% from the beginning of the year. The capital quality of commercial banks maintained a relatively high level when compared with their foreign peers. Common shares comprised over 80% of the total, and the leverage ratio was kept in a globally safe range. Moody's Investors Service raised China's sovereign rating outlook from "stable" to "positive". The banking industry enjoyed increasingly stronger anti-risk capability and accordingly a higher international reputation. As of the end of 2009, the banking financial institutions posted a total asset of RMB 78.8 trillion (+26.3% YoY).

The Capital Market Saw Innovative Progress and Market System Construction Made a Great Step Forward

In 2009, China's capital market maintained generally sound development and its functions were better manifested. The reforms in the direct financing market were carried out at an accelerated pace and new shares issuance was resumed. The year saw nine companies listed on the main board, 90 companies traded on the SME board and growth enterprise market (GEM), refinancing by 150 listed companies, M&A by 56 companies and overseas listing of six companies. The domestic capital market saw a full-year financing amount of RMB 446.6 billion, the second highest level in history. Iron & steel, auto, coal and other industries achieved or are achieving the goal of industrial integration, upgrading or state-owned economic layout adjustment through M&A and reorganization. The launch of GEM offered new financing channels for companies featuring independent innovation and growing startups. The futures market boasted rapidly increasing categories and registered a turnover of RMB 130.5 trillion (+81.5% YoY), showing a better capability in serving companies related to the industrial chain. Stock indices generally went up and the turnover increased. Shanghai Composite Index and Shenzhen Composite Index rose by 80% and 111% in 2009. Shanghai and Shenzhen stock exchanges saw an accumulated turnover of RMB 58.2 trillion (+62.4% YoY).

The Insurance Industry Developed Rapidly and Healthily and Had Closer Ties with the Capital Market

China's insurance industry vigorously combated the financial crisis, pushed for regulatory innovation and promoted scientific development in an orderly manner. That led to better-than-expected business development, effective prevention of industrial risks, positive progress in structural adjustment, better market orders and economic benefits as well as evidently enhancing overall strength. At the end of 2009, the insurance companies owned RMB 4.1 trillion of total assets and RMB 460.48 billion of net assets (+RMB 144.18 billion YoY). The insurance fund application balance reached RMB 3.7 trillion. The funds utilization earnings stood at RMB 214.17 billion, and the ROI was 6.41% (+4.5% YoY). The barriers between the mutual investment and in-depth cooperation between banks and insurance companies were removed and the investment channels for insurance funds were expanded step by step. The role of the insurance industry in the financial systems was further strengthened.

Column 1

The Stimulus Package Designed to Cope with the International Financial Crisis

The international financial crisis broke out in September 2008 and quickly spread to the rest of the world. China's economy was heavily impacted and the social and economic development faced severe challenges. Based on accurate judgment of the situations, the CPC Central Committee and State Council timely launched ten measures intended to further expand domestic demand and promote stable and fast economic growth in early November. Proactive fiscal policies and moderately loose monetary policies were resolutely adopted, and government investment was increased by a big margin to help implement a two-year investment plan involving RMB 4 trillion. In 2009, China further developed a series of policies that combine both long-term and short-term goals and highlight solutions for both symptoms and root causes to beef up fiscal and monetary support, expand both domestic and external demand, revitalize key industries, intensify scientific & technological support, foster emerging industries and improve social security. That gave rise to a package plan aimed at tackling the financial crisis and fueling fast and sound economic growth.

Column 2

Release and Implementation of the Newly Revised Insurance Law

On February 28, 2009, the Seventh Session of the 11th National People's Congress passed the draft of the revised *Insurance Law of the People's Republic of China*, which was implemented as of October 1, 2009. The new law was improved in such aspects as the legal norms for insurance contracts, basic systems of the insurance industry and insurance regulation when compared with the previous one. It also places greater emphasis on protecting the interests of insurants, further regularizes detailed insurance practices and strengthens investigation into illegal acts. The launch of the new insurance law was an important event in China's insurance history. It signifies the further maturity of China's insurance legal systems and exerts positive and far-reaching influence upon the whole insurance industry.

Column 3

Commercial Banks Approved to Take a Stake in Insurance Companies

On January 16, 2008, China Banking Regulatory Commission and China Insurance Regulatory Commission signed *The MOU on Strengthening In-depth Cooperation between Banking and Insurance Industry as well as Inter-industrial Regulatory Cooperation* which allowed banks and insurance companies to carry out pilot programs of mutual investment under the principle of market orientation, equality and mutual benefit. On November 26, 2009, China Banking Regulatory Commission officially released *The Notice on Issuing the Pilot Administrative Measures for Commercial Banks to Make Equity Investment in Insurance Companies* which put forward detailed criteria for pilot institutions in terms of access conditions, application procedures, risk control and regulation management. The pilot launch of commercial banks' taking a stake in insurance companies will facilitate the resource sharing and strengthen complementarity between banks and insurance companies and better satisfy consumers' increasingly growing need in diverse financial services.

03

Insurance Industry Serves the Construction of a Harmonious Society

- Promoting Steady and Fast Economic Growth
- Serving the Work Related to Agriculture, Farmers and Rural Areas
- Participation in the Construction of a Multi-level Social Security System
- Maintaining Social Harmony and Stability

By thoroughly implementing the scientific outlook on development and adhering to the guideline of "doing own job well and serving overall situations" in 2009, the insurance industry played a positive role in securing steady economic growth, improving the people's livelihood and maintaining social stability.

Insurance Industry Serves the Construction of a Harmonious Society

Promoting Steady and Fast Economic Growth

The insurance industry earnestly implemented the measures designed by the State Council to stabilize external demand and boost domestic demand, and energetically developed credit insurance and guarantee insurance. In 2009, the value of credit insurance for domestic and foreign trade totaled RMB 911.46 billion (+82.6% YoY). Specifically speaking, the short-term credit insurance value stood at USD 90.27 billion on a cumulative basis (+2.2 times YoY), surpassing the goal of USD 84.00 billion set by the State Council. Export finance insurance programs for large-scale complete sets of equipment numbered 86 involving a contract value of USD30.5 billion, six times that of 2008. The penetration rate of export credit insurance in China's general export rose to 18.6% from 6.5% in 2008. Active efforts were also made to serve the country's revitalization plan for ten key industries and push forward pilot programs of new-type car loan insurance, small loan guarantee insurance and science & technology insurance, and guarantee insurance value which amounted to RMB 229.99 billion.

Serving the Work Related to Agriculture, Farmers and Rural Areas

The coverage of agricultural insurance expanded steadily. In 2009, China's agricultural insurance registered a premium of RMB 13.39 billion (+21% YoY), offering a risk protection of RMB 381.21 billion (+59% YoY) and protecting 133 million farm families (+47.9% YoY). Crop farming insurance covered 950 million mu (633.3 trillon square meters) of crops and forests. Livestock breeding insurance covered 69.46 million domestic animals and 610 million fowl. The accumulated compensation pay-outs of agricultural insurance reached RMB 9.52 billion, benefiting 18.23 million farm families.

The scope of insurance liabilities kept widening. Drought as well as pest and disease damage to the farmers that was frequently reported were included in the coverage of crop planting insurance. All the animal diseases (epidemics), natural disasters, contingencies and government culling were basically covered by livestock breeding insurance. At present, the risks covered by China's agricultural insurance are even more extensive than those in developed countries.

The insurance coverage continued to expand. In 2009, the types of insurance subsidized by the central finance ministry were extended to nine which included fattening pig breeding insurance and forest insurance. At present, there were more than 160 types of rural insurance available nationwide covering a wide range of aspects related to the issues of agriculture, farmers and rural areas from crop planting, livestock breeding, farmers' lives to rural family property and life in old age. Up to 20 insurance companies offered a variety of agricultural insurance. The agricultural insurance operation networks consisting of national insurance companies and professional insurance companies initially took shape, and the agricultural insurance covered every province and municipality across the country.

Pilot microinsurance programs were advanced smoothly in rural areas. While highlighting the development of agricultural insurance, the insurance industry kept innovating service modes and expanding insurance coverage. As of the end of 2009, pilot microinsurance has been extended to 19 provinces and autonomous regions and registered a premium of RMB 230 million offering a risk protection of RMB 136.4 billion for 8.71 million people.

Participation in the Construction of a Multi-level Social Security System

Participation in medical & health system reform: By implementing *The Opinion of the CPC Central Committee and the State Council on Deepening the Reform in China's Medical and Health System* and participating in the construction of the social medical security system, the insurance industry has offered 160 million recipients basic medical and complementary medical insurance services. Effort was also made to win support of relevant authorities to push forward the progress of pilot programs of income tax-deferred pension insurance in Shanghai.

Expansion of health insurance coverage: By the end of 2009, the insurance industry provided health risk coverage of RMB 28.5 trillion for 1.3 billion recipients and paid a compensation value of RMB 21.7 billion. Meanwhile, the health insurance entrustment management business expanded steadily, and the full-year newly added mandatory management funds totaled RMB 6.96 billion providing compensation and reimbursement services for 18.90 million recipients and the compensation value was RMB 8.68 billion.

Further expansion of pension insurance coverage: By the end of 2009, a total of 11.63 million recipients were offered commercial pension risk coverage. Corporate annuity business grew rapidly providing annuity insurance services for 67.63 million recipients, up 13% from the beginning of the year. Pension insurance companies collected an annuity trust fee of RMB 26.36 billion, up 28.3% from the beginning of the year; The assets managed under trust reached RMB 70.8 billion, and assets managed as investment totaled RMB 48.61 billion, up 49.5% and 28.8% respectively from early 2009.

Maintaining Social Harmony and Stability

Vigorous effort was made to push for the development of liability insurance in such fields as medical care, transportation, education and environmental protection. The liability insurance for environmental pollution has been piloted in eight provinces and municipalities. Medical liability insurance has been initiated in 56 cities across 16 provinces, municipalities and autonomous regions and it serves as an important measure of the Central Committee for Comprehensive Management of Public Security for building safe hospitals and plays a big role in settling doctor-patient disputes and sharing medical liability risks. Positive efforts were also made to guide relevant companies in properly managing the medical compensation funds for babies sickened by contaminated milk powder and doing a good job in the claim settlement involved in the snow disaster in Northeast China and some other regions. The insurance regulator also joined hands with relevant ministries and commissions issuing 13 guidance documents aimed at promoting business development and better serving the economic and social lives of the people. In 2009, the insurance industry provided a liability risk coverage of RMB 69.2 trillion and made a compensation payment of RMB 3.9 billion. Specifically, it paid RMB 1.78 billion, RMB 250 million, RMB 1.09 billion and RMB 620 million in compensation funds for public liability, product liability, employer liability and professional liability respectively playing a good role in social management.

Column 4

Commercial Insurance's Participation in the Construction of the Medical Security System

In 2009, the CPC Central Committee and State Council issued *The Opinion on Deepening the Reform in China's Medical and Health System and The Implementation Plan for the Recent Priorities of the Health Care System Reform (2009-2011)*. The documents specified the guideline, fundamental principles, general goals and major measures for the reform of China's medical and health system. It put forward the construction of a multi-level medical security system that covers both urban and rural residents, and fully affirmed the vital role of commercial health insurance in China's medical security system which are of great guiding significance to the development of the insurance industry both in the short run and long run. On May 27, 2009, China Insurance Regulatory Commission released *The Opinions on the Insurance Industry's Further Implementation of the Medical Reform Opinions and Active Participation in the Establishment of a Multi-level Medical Security System* which offered the insurance industry specific guiding opinions in terms of how to implement the new medical reform plans.

Column 5

Implementation of the No.2 Interpretations for Enterprise Accounting Standards

The Ministry of Finance issued the *No.2 Interpretations for Enterprise Accounting Standards (No.2 Interpretations)* on August 7, 2008, requiring both domestic and overseas listed companies to adopt the same accounting policies and accounting estimates for the same transaction in confirming, computation and reporting. China Insurance Regulatory Commission released *The Circular on the Insurance Industry Effectively Fulfilling the No. 2 Interpretations for Enterprise Accounting Standards on January* 5, 2009, requiring all the insurance companies listed either at home or abroad to follow the new accounting policies and to alter the accounting policies that caused differences between domestic and overseas accounting statements when compiling financial reports for 2009. The implementation of the No.2 Interpretations will exert significant influence upon insurance companies in a wide range of aspects like accounting, audits, internal control, corporate governance and development strategies. It will facilitate the objective and impartial reflection of the financial status and economic achievements of insurance companies and further promote the restructuring as well as the rapid and sound development of the insurance industry.

04

Further Improvement of the Insurance Regulatory System

- Responsibilities of China Insurance Regulatory Commission
- Organizational Structure of the CIRC
- Objectives of Supervision
- Further Maturation of the Insurance Regulatory Concept
- Further Optimization and Integration of Regulatory Resources
- Further Implementation of Regulatory Laws and Regulations
- Continuous Innovation in Off-site Regulation Approaches
- Actually Intensified Market Behavior Regulation
- Effective Prevention of Industrial Risks

On November 18, 1998, the China Insurance Regulatory Commission (hereinafter referred to as CIRC) was established. After that, it successively set up branches in 29 provincial capitals. From 2004 onwards, it added local offices in 6 cities specifically designated in the state plan. Currently, it has insurance regulatory institutions in all provincial capitals with the exception of Tibet. By the end of 2009, there were 2,550 persons working for the national insurance regulation, including 387 in CIRC offices and 2,163 in branches.

Further Improvement of the Insurance Regulatory System

Responsibilities of China Insurance Regulatory Commission

The CIRC's main responsibilities

1 Formulating policies, strategies and plans regarding the development of the insurance industry, drafting relevant laws and regulations regarding insurance supervision ad regulation, and making relevant rules for the insurance industry.

2 Examining and approving the establishment of insurance companies and their branches, insurance groups and insurance holding companies; approving in conjunction with relevant authorities the establishment of insurance asset management companies; examining and approving the establishment of representative offices by overseas insurance organizations within the territory of the People's Republic of China; examining and approving the establishment of insurance intermediaries such as agencies, brokerages, loss-adjusting companies and their branches; examining and approving the establishment of overseas insurance organizations by domestic insurance and non-insurance organizations; examining and approving the merger, split, alteration and dissolution of insurance organizations; deciding whether or not to take over an insurance company or designating an organization to take it over; organizing or participating in the bankruptcy and liquidation process of insurance companies.

3 Examining and confirming the qualifications of senior managerial personnel in all insurance-related organizations; establishing the basic qualification standards for insurance practitioners.

4 Examining and approving the clauses and premium rates of insurance lines related to public interests, statutory insurance lines and newly developed life insurance lines; filing the insurance clauses and premium rates of the other insurance lines.

5 Supervising the solvency and market conduct of insurance companies according to law; managing the insurance security fund, and monitoring the insurance guarantee deposits; formulating rules and regulations on insurance fund management on the basis of laws and relevant policies of the State, and supervising insurance fund management according to law.

6 Supervising the business operation of public-policy-oriented insurance and statutory insurance; supervising organizational forms and operations such as captive insurance and mutual insurance; conducting administration of societies and organizations such as China Insurance Association and China Insurance Society.

7 Conducting investigation into the following irregularities and imposing penalties accordingly: unfair competition and other irregularities by insurance organizations and practitioners, direct engagement or disguised engagement in insurance business by non-insurance organizations.

8 Supervising overseas insurance organizations established by domestic insurance and non-insurance organizations according to law.

9 Laying down standards for the information system of the insurance industry; establishing insurance risk-assessment, risk-warning and risk-monitoring systems; following, analyzing, monitoring and predicting the operation of the insurance market; compiling the statistics and report forms of the insurance industry and disclosing them in accordance with relevant regulations of the State.

10 Taking on other duties commissioned by the State Council.

Organizational Structure of the CIRC

Chairman

Vice Chairman

Vice Chairman

Vice Chairman

Vice Chairman

Secretary of Discipline

Assistant Chairman

Assistant Chairman

- General Office
- Development and Reform Department
- Policy Research Department
- Finance and Accounting Department
- Property Insurance Regulatory Department
- Life Insurance Regulatory Department
- Insurance Intermediary Regulatory Department
- Insurance Fund Management Regulatory Department
- International Department
- Legal Affairs Department
- Statistics and IT Department
- Inspection Bureau
- Personnel and Education Department
- Disciplinary Inspection Department
- Party Committee of CIRC Head Office

35 local offices, directly affiliated to CIRC, are authorized to administer, supervise and regulate local insurance markets, to ensure that the local insurance market operates in a sound and compliant manner, and to guide local insurance industry's sustained, rapid, orderly and healthy development.

Objectives of Supervision

- To protect the interests of policyholders
- To facilitate the sustained, rapid and orderly development of China's insurance industry
- To safeguard against and resolve industry risks

Further Maturation of the Insurance Regulatory Concept

Adhering to scientific regulatory concepts, the insurance regulators continued to improve the legal system for regulation which consisted of the regulatory system supported by the three pillars (market behavior, solvency and corporate governance) and the five defense lines for preventing risks. They placed consistent emphasis on the prevention of risks, the transformation of development mode, and the protection of insurants' interests. They worked to solve the structural and institutional problems that restricted the stable and healthy development of the insurance industry, and increasingly made the regulation more scientific, effective and targeted.

Further Optimization and Integration of Regulatory Resources

The organizational structures of the regulatory institutions were improved, and the Inspection Bureau and the Training Center were set up. Effort was also made to further define the regulatory responsibilities, beef up investigation into illegal acts, strengthen the education for regulatory groups and enhance the level of scientific regulation. Pilot programs of territorial regulation for insurance corporate entities were kicked off. The single pattern of CIRC directly assuming regulatory functions was gradually replaced by the regulatory mechanism in which the regulation work is collaborated between CIRC and its local branches – namely the former offers guidance and the latter implements it.

Further Implementation of Regulatory Laws and Regulations

Based on the implementation of the revised Insurance Law, effort was made to do a thorough job in abolishing and revising previous regulations and establishing new ones as well as to revise and release seven regulatory frameworks including *The Regulations on Administration of Insurance Companies: The Regulations on the Management of Qualifications of Directors, Supervisors and Senior Executives in Insurance Companies and The Measures for the Punishment of Illegal Acts in the Intermediary Business of Insurance Companies.* Those frameworks helped improve the institutional systems for insurance regulation and operation and helped broadly push forward the regulation and operation according to law. Effort was also made to improve the regulation for governance structure, set up the Regulatory Commission for the Governance of Insurance Companies, launch the policy of issuing vehicle insurance policy upon payment, popularize the "zero-cash" payment system for life insurance and establish the system

for online enquiry of insurance underwriting and claim settlement information. The system for the standard operation of the life insurance market was intensified and the regulatory systems concerning new-type product information disclosure, operational criteria for life accident insurance business and insurance purchase were promptly established. The regulators also strengthened corporate entity regulation, beefed up capital constraint, embarked on the revision of minimum capital amount, built risk prompting and notifying systems and developed internal risk isolation system for insurance groups.

Continuous Innovation in Off-site Regulation Approaches

The regulators continued to intensify solvency regulation, improve solvency regulation mechanisms, enrich the criteria for solvency regulation and strengthen the rigid constraints for solvency regulation. Measures were taken to help 45 companies raise RMB 22.5 billion of capital, help ten companies issue RMB 18 billion of subordinated debts and urge unqualified companies to improve their solvency conditions and reduce capital consumption. Classified regulation was advanced steadily based on improved classified regulation methods and working mechanisms. Class C and D companies were taken as the primary targets for regulation and 42 regulation measures were adopted, which basically enabled the organic combination of classified regulation and solvency regulation. The construction of regulation informatization was strengthened and the information-based platform was initially completed, basically covering all the major fields of the off-site regulation.

Actually Intensified Market Behavior Regulation

The regulators further standardized the insurance market, conducted inspections of data authenticity, regulated bank insurance businesses and short-term accident insurance businesses. They intensified investigation into illegal intermediary services offered by insurance companies, cracked down on illegal practices such as fund-raising fraud and misappropriation of premiums and further drove forward the campaign of fighting fake insurance companies, fake policies and fake insurance claims. In 2009, the regulators investigated and punished 32 cases of fake insurance institutions and 16,000 cases of fake insurance claims which in all involved a premium amount of more than RMB 100 million and a compensation amount of RMB 420 million. 298 cases involving 442 persons were transferred to judicial authorities, 976 administrative punishments were made to insurance institutions, including 51 insurance companies that were stopped from receiving new business and 35 in which business licenses were revoked; a total of 113 senior executives were dismissed or replaced. Institutions and individuals involved in the cases were fined RMB 42.41 million and RMB 5.97 million respectively.

Effective Prevention of Industrial Risks

Facing the international financial crisis, the regulators actively adopted a series of measures to improve risk prevention mechanisms, highlight key factors in risk prevention, intensify international cooperation in regulation and enhance the industry's risk prevention capability in an all-round way. This effectively prevented cross-border risk transmission and various sorts of new risks as well as positively solve the problems left over by history and ensure safe and steady industrial operation. By the end of 2009, there were eight insurance companies that failed to meet the solvency criteria – five less than the number in early 2009. Capital utilization regulation was further intensified and the insurance asset allocation was brought into a balance either by safety, liquidity or profitability.

Column 6

Crackdown on Fake Insurance Institutions, Fake Policies and Fake Claims

Intensified effort was made to crack down on fake insurance institutions, fake policies and fake claims ("Three Fakes"), which served as a crucial measure adopted by CIRC 2009 to strengthen insurance regulation and prevent and reduce risks. Under the guidance of CIRC, the whole industry made vigorous efforts to eliminate potential risks and investigated several "Three Fakes" cases. As a result, a mechanism for law enforcement coordination among multiple authorities came into shape and remarkable progress was achieved in the campaign of cracking down on "Three Fakes". In 2009, China's insurance industry saw 32 cases of fake insurance institutions and 16,000 cases of fake claims that involved a premium amount of RMB 100 million and above and a compensation amount of RMB 420 million.

Column 7

Classified Regulation Implemented by the Regulatory Institutions

CIRC began to explore classified regulation in life insurance and property insurance in 2006 and 2007 with a view to making insurance regulation more scientific, targeted and effective as well as efficiently prevent and reduce risks. Based on pilot programs and a summary of experiences, CIRC devised a new system for classified regulation and decided to formally implement classified regulation for property and life insurance companies as well as insurance intermediary companies as of January 1, 2009. Classified regulation is a kind of comprehensive regulation approach aimed at risk control. At the beginning of every year, CIRC will assess and classify all the insurance companies based on the audited data of the previous year and determine regulatory measures targeted at different types of companies. Then, it will assess quarterly data and make corresponding adjustments concerning annual assessment results and regulatory measures. Due to the large number of insurance intermediary agencies, the regulators will implement dynamic regulation, assess risks in a real-time manner and adopt differentiated regulatory measures based on actual situations.

05

Insurance Market Operation

- Business of Non-life Insurance Companies
- Business of Life Insurance Companies
- Professional Reinsurance Business
- Insurance Intermediary Market
- Foreign Insurance Business
- Insurance Assets Management

In 2009, China's insurance industry achieved a total premium of RMB 1113.73 billion (+13.8% YoY). The insurance penetration was 3.32%[①] (+0.07% YoY) and the insurance density was RMB 834.4 (+RMB 97.7 YoY). The indemnity and compensation pay-outs amounted to RMB 312.55 billion (+5.2% YoY). The total assets of insurance companies reached RMB 4.1 trillion (+21.6% from the beginning of 2009). There were eight Insurance Group Companies, 120 insurance companies (+8 YoY) and nine insurance asset management companies.
Following the execution of the No.2 Interpretation of Accounting Standards for Business Enterprise, the insurance industry recorded a total insurance revenue of RMB 1005.74 billion in 2009 (+27.2% YoY). Specifically, the non-life insurance companies achieved a insurance revenue of RMB 300.12 billion (+22.3% YoY), life insurance companies RMB 667.62 billion (+29.3% YoY), and reinsurance companies RMB 38 billion (+33% YoY).

Insurance Market Operation

Business of Non-life Insurance Companies

Steady and Fast Growth of Premium

The non-life insurance businesses continued the strong momentum of growth in 2009, achieving a premium of RMB 299.29 billion (+22.4% YoY), a growth rate 5.1% higher than that of 2008.

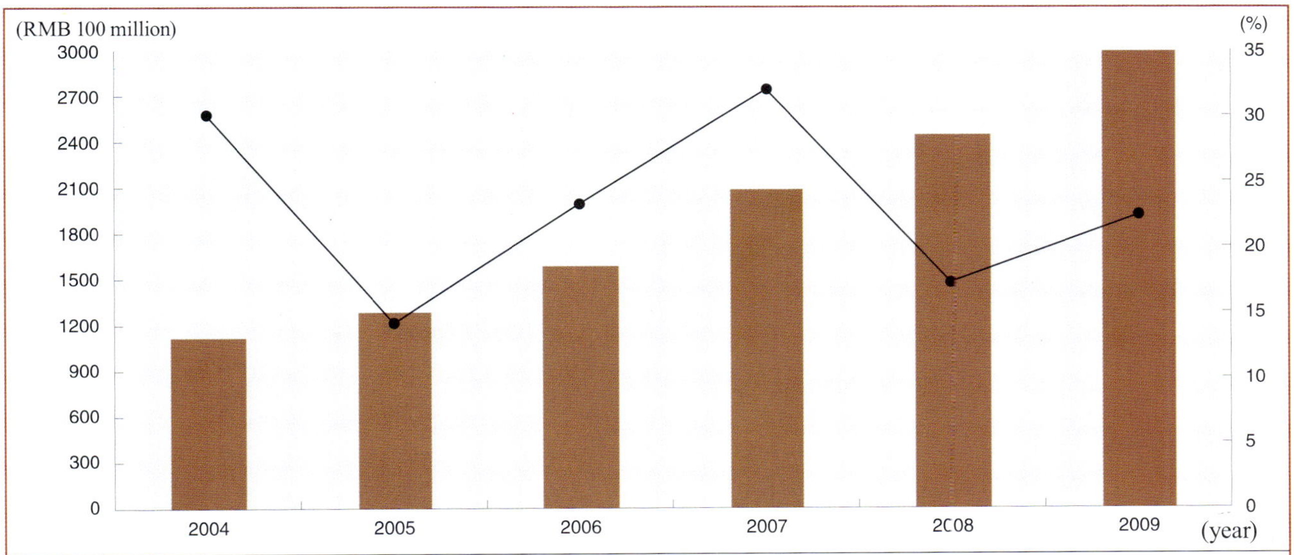

		2004	2005	2006	2007	2008	2009
Premium	(left scale)	1124.8	1283.5	1581.1	2086.6	2446.2	2992.9
Growth rate	(right scale)	30.0	14.1	23.2	32.0	17.3	22.4

Figure 2 Premium and Growth Rate of Non-life Insurance Companies during 2004–2009

Top 5 contributors of premium consisted of vehicle insurance, corporate property insurance, agricultural insurance, liability insurance and accident insurance, which accounted for 89.5% of the total premium.

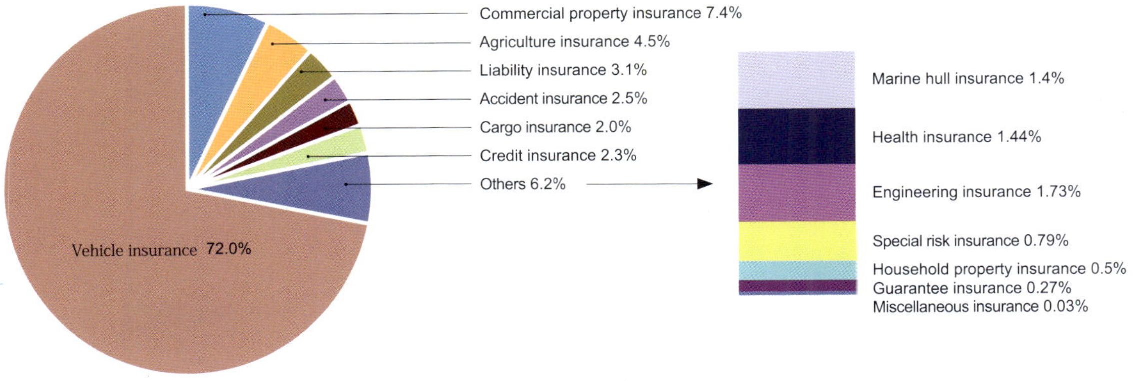

Figure 3 Premium Structure of Non-life Insurance Business in 2009

① The insurance penetration and insurance density were figured out according to the premium data based on the business statistical approach.

Most of the non-life insurance types registered stable growth including vehicle insurance (+26.6% YoY), household property insurance (+19.1% YoY), agricultural insurance (+21% YoY), liability insurance (+12.8% YoY), engineering insurance (+31.6% YoY) and health insurance (+17.1% YoY), and the credit insurance premium grew by 91.3% YoY.

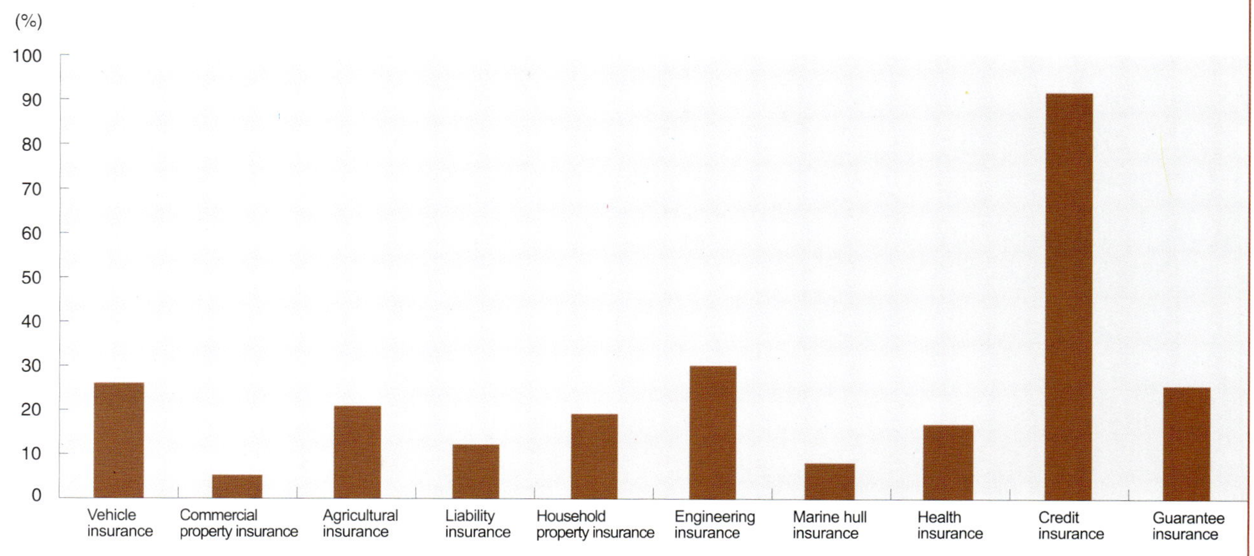

Note: Others include household property insurance, credit insurance, surety bond insurance, accident insurance, marine hull and special risk insurance, etc.

Figure 4 Premium Growth of Major Non-life Insurance Types in 2009

Table 1 Top 10 Non-life Insurance Companies by Premium in 2009

Rank	Name	Capital structure	Premium (RMB 100 million)	Market share (%)
1	PICC Property and Casualty Company Limited	Domestic	1194.6	39.9
2	Ping An Insurance (Group) Company of China, Ltd.	Domestic	384.8	12.9
3	China Pacific Insurance (Group) Co., Ltd.	Domestic	342.3	11.4
4	China United Insurance Holding Company Limited	Domestic	194.4	6.5
5	China Continent Property & Casualty Insurance Company Ltd.	Domestic	102.5	3.4
6	China Life Property and Casualty Insurance Company Limited.	Domestic	79.1	2.6
7	Tian An Insurance Co., Ltd.	Domestic	70.0	2.3
8	China Export & Credit Insurance Corporation	Domestic	68.4	2.3
9	Sunshine Property and Casualty Insurance Co., Ltd.	Domestic	66.0	2.2
10	Yong An Property Insurance Co., Ltd.	Domestic	53.4	1.8
	Total		2555.5	85.3

Market Players Increased Steadily while Market Concentration Further Decreased

By the end of 2009, China had 52 non-life insurance companies, including 34 domestic-funded companies, 18 foreign-funded companies and five newly added non-life insurance companies.

The non-life insurance market concentration continued to decline; with the top five insurance companies by premium comprising 74.1% (-1.5% YoY) of the market share.

Compensation Pay-outs Continued to Rise

In 2009, non-life insurance companies paid total compensation pay-outs of RMB 163.82 billion (+11.0% YoY) and the growth rate decreased by 28.1% on a year-on-year basis. The compensation pay-outs grew (on a year-on-year basis) in vehicle insurance (+14.7%), commercial property insurance (-27.6%), household property insurance (-20.7%), engineering insurance (+24.4%), liability insurance (+17.7%), credit insurance (+82.8%), agricultural insurance (+48.4%) and health insurance (+19.3%). In 2009, the overall expense ratio of earned premium of non-life insurance companies reached 38.2%.

Reserve Balance Continued to Grow

By the end of 2009, the undue liability reserves and outstanding loss reserves of non-life insurance companies reached RMB 243 billion (+18.8% YoY) including undue liability reserves of RMB 129.82 billion and outstanding loss reserves of RMB 113.18 billion.

In 2009, non-life insurance companies withdrew undue liability reserves of RMB 23.23 billion and outstanding loss reserves of RMB 15.15 billion.

Column 8

Insurance Companies Made Significant Progress in Institutional Reform

In 2009, China's insurance industry continued to regard the institutional reform as a fundamental and strategic work and made further advances in restructuring and listing. The People's Insurance Company of China (PICC) successfully accomplished the overall restructuring and was formally incorporated as a joint-stock group in October 2009. China Pacific Insurance (Group) Co., Ltd. (CPIC) successfully went public in Hong Kong becoming the fourth domestic insurance company traded overseas. China Export & Credit Insurance Corporation vigorously advanced its institutional reform.

Column 9

Credit Insurance Helped Stabilize External Demand

In 2009, China strived to improve its policies regarding export credit insurance and made it a crucial means of stabilizing external demand with a view to reducing the impact of the global financial crisis upon China's foreign trade. The insurance industry actively served the overall growth of both society and economy and energetically developed export credit insurance. In 2009, China Export & Credit Insurance Corporation achieved a credit insurance and guarantee insurance value of USD116.6 billion (+85.8% YoY). The penetration rate of export credit insurance in China's general exports rose to 18.6% from 6.5% in 2008 playing an important role in stabilizing China's exports.

Business of Life Insurance Companies[1]

Stable Growth of Premium

In 2009, life insurance companies realized a premium of RMB 814.42 billion (+11.0% YoY) accounting for 73.1% of gross national premium.

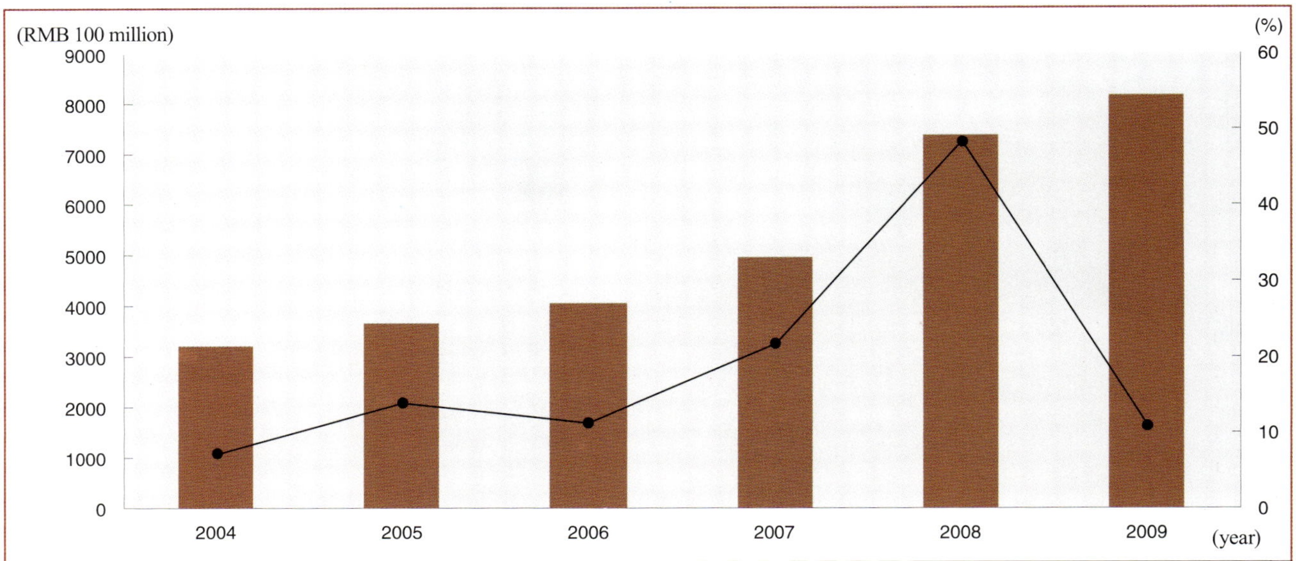

		2004	2005	2006	2007	2008	2009
Premium	(left scale)	3198.2	3644.9	4059.1	4946.5	7342.6	8144.2
Growth rate	(right scale)	7.2	14.0	11.3	21.9	48.5	11.0

Figure 5 Premium and Growth Rate of Life Insurance Companies during 2004–2009

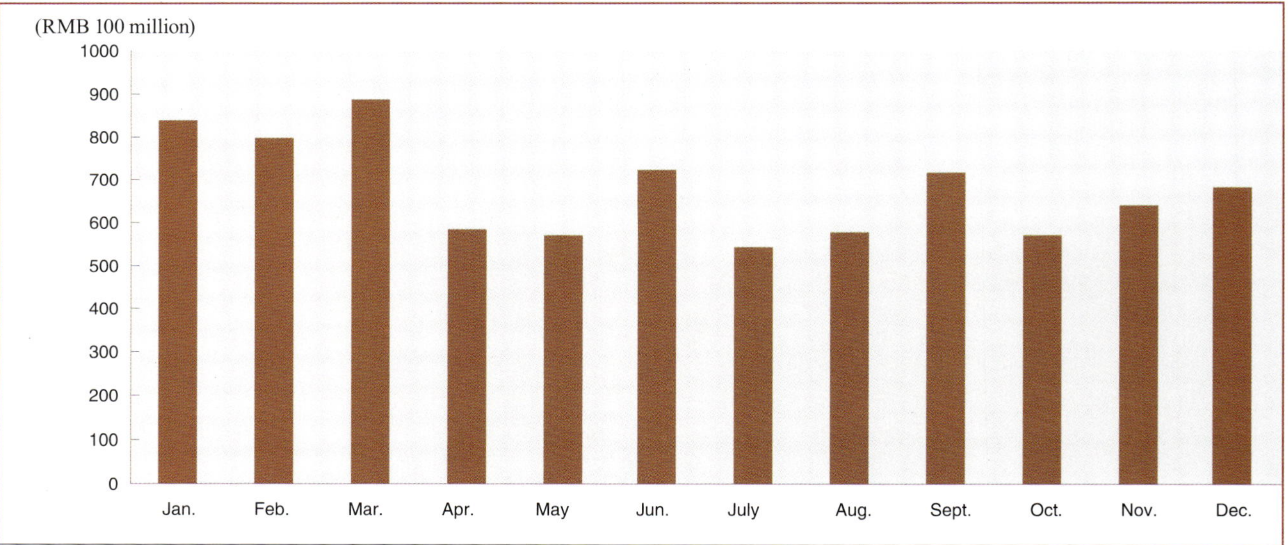

	Jan.	Feb.	Mar.	Apr.	May	Jun.	July	Aug.	Sept.	Oct.	Nov.	Dec.
Premium	839	800	886	589	575	720	545	576	719	573	642	680

Figure 6 Monthly Premium of Life Insurance Companies in 2009

Business Structure Continued to Optimize

By the end of 2009, the premium of new life insurance policies reached RMB 542.64 billion (+4.8% YoY) accounting for 66.6% of the total premium of life insurance companies. The premium equivalent of new policies stood at RMB 172.14 billion (+19.5% YoY). The installment premium of new policies amounted to RMB 136.51 billion (+33.4% YoY) comprising 25.2% of the premium of new policies of life insurance companies (the proportion rose by 5.4%). Ten-year-and-above installment premiums increased by 22.7% on a year-on-year basis.

① Including specialist health insurance companies and pension insurance companies.

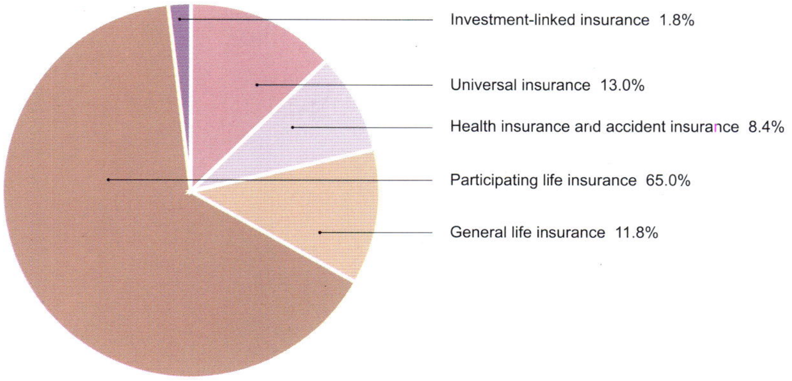

Figure 7 Premium Structure of Life Insurance Business in 2009

Rapid Growth of Premium of Participating Life Insurance

In 2009, the participating life insurance registered a premium of RMB 529.26 billion (+39.3% YoY) making up 65% (+13.2% YoY) of the total premium of life insurance and playing an important role in stabilizing the growth of the premium of life insurance companies.

The premium of universal insurance business was RMB 105.52 billion (-27.3% YoY) accounting for 13% of the total premium of life insurance companies (-6.8% YoY). The premium of investment-linked insurance reached RMB 14.79 billion (-65.2% YoY) and made up 1.8% of the total (-4% YoY). The premium of general life insurance totaled RMB 96.16 billion (-2.3% YoY) and represented 11.8% of the total (-1.6% YoY).

The combined premium of health insurance and accident insurance amounted to RMB 68.7 billion (+1.1% YoY) and comprised 8.4% of the total (-0.8% YoY).

Stable Development of Personal Life Insurance Marketing and Bank & Post Office Channels

Personal marketing channel realized a premium of RMB 356.93 billion (+15.8% YoY) accounting for 43.8% of the total life insurance premium.

Bank and post office channel realized a premium of RMB 388.59 billion (+8.2% YoY) accounting for 47.7% of the total life insurance premium.

Corporate direct sales channel realized a premium of RMB 53.90 billion (-7.8% YoY) accounting for 6.6% of the total life insurance premium.

Insurance brokerage channel realized a premium of RMB 1.61 billion (+12.9% YoY). Specialist agent channel realized a premium of RMB 5.92 billion (+30.8% YoY).

Slight increase in the Number of Market Players

By the end of 2009, there were 59 personal insurance companies in China including 50 life insurance companies, five professional pension insurance companies and four professional health insurance companies. The total number was three more than that of 2008. Specifically, domestic-funded companies numbered 31 (including Aeon Life and China Post Life and not including Huatai Life), and foreign-funded companies numbered 28 (including HSBC Life and Huatai Life).

The top five companies by premium accounted for 77.1% of the market share (-1.5% YoY).

Table 2 Top 10 Life Insurance Companies by Premium in 2009

Rank	Name	Capital Structure	Premium (RMB 100 million)	Market Share (%)
1	China Life Insurance Company Ltd.	Domestic	2950.4	36.2
2	Ping An Life Insurance Company Of China, Ltd.	Domestic	1323.0	16.2
3	China Pacific Life Insurance Co., Ltd.	Domestic	675.8	8.3
4	Tai Kang Life Insurance Co., Ltd.	Domestic	670.1	8.2
5	New China Life Insurance Co., Ltd.	Domestic	667.8	8.2
6	PICC Life Insurance Company Limited.	Domestic	524.4	6.4
7	Tai Ping Life Insurance Co., Ltd.	Domestic	225.9	2.8
8	American International Assurance Company Limited	Foreign-owned	80.4	1.0
9	Sino Life Insurance Co., Ltd.	Domestic	70.0	0.9
10	PICC Health Insurance Company Limited	Domestic	62.0	0.8
	Total		7249.8	89.0

Stable Surrender Value of Life Insurance①

In 2009, life insurance companies surrendered an insurance premium of RMB 106.97 billion (+10.7% YoY), and the surrender ratio was 3.54% (-0.3% YoY). Specifically, domestic-funded life insurance companies posted a surrender ratio of 3.43% and foreign-funded companies 5.65%.

Slight Decline in Indemnity and Compensation Pay-outs

Life insurance companies recorded RMB 148.7 billion (-0.6% YoY) of various types of indemnity and compensation pay-outs.

Table 3 Life Insurance Companies' Indemnity and Compensation Pay-outs in 2009

Type	Indemnity and Compensation Pay-outs（RMB 100 million）	Growth Rate YOY (%)	Percentage Share (%)
Life insurance	1268.5	-3.5	85.3
Health insurance	182.8	24.7	12.3
Accident insurance	35.7	4.7	2.4
Total	1487.0	-0.6	100.0

Professional Reinsurance Business

By the end of 2009, there was one reinsurance (group) company which was China Reinsurance (Group) Corporation. There were also nine professional reinsurance companies including China Property & Casualty Reinsurance Company Ltd., China Life Reinsurance Company Ltd., Munich Re Beijing Branch, Swiss Re Beijing Branch, Cologne Re Shanghai Branch, Lloyd's China, Scor China, Hannover Re Shanghai Branch and China International Reinsurance Company Limited Beijing Branch.

In 2009, the total reinsurance premium of China's reinsurance companies reached RMB 43.33 billion (+4.7% YoY). The total reinsurance compensation pay-outs of nationwide reinsurance companies totaled RMB 23.63 billion (+34.2% YoY).

Insurance Intermediary Market

In 2009, the premium achieved through various insurance intermediary channels reached RMB 916.11 billion② (+13.9% YoY) accounting for 82.3% of the national total.

Table 4 Premium and Percentage of Various Insurance Intermediary Channels in 2009

Sales Channel	Insurance Agencies	Insurance Brokers	Cross-Sector Intermediaries	Insurance Sales Representatives	Total
Premium (RMB 100 million）	328.9	244.7	4460.7	4126.9	9161.1
Growth rate YoY（%）	21.9	-0.3	7.5	22.1	13.9
Percentage（%）	3.0	2.2	40.1	37.1	82.3

Professional Insurance Intermediaries

In 2009, there were 2,570 (+125 YoY) professional insurance intermediaries in China, including 1,903 insurance agencies, 378 insurance brokers and 289 surveyors and loss adjusters.

In 2009, the total operating income of nationwide professional insurance intermediaries reached RMB 8.92 billion (+24.9% YoY). Specifically, professional insurance agencies achieved an agent fees income of RMB 4.48 billion (+33.7% YoY). Insurance brokers achieved an operating income of RMB 3.31 billion (+24.9% YoY). Surveyors and loss adjusters achieved an operating income of RMB 1.13 billion (-0.96% YoY).

① The surrender value and surrender ratio were data based on the business statistical approach.

② Part of the data came from the statements submitted to relevant insurance regulatory authorities by insurance companies and professional insurance intermediary agencies.

Cross-sector Insurance Intermediaries

By the end of 2009, there were 148,971 (+9% YoY) cross-sector insurance intermediaries nationwide and the agent fees income totaled RMB 22.21 billion (+24.6% YoY).

Table 5 Business Structure of Cross-sector Insurance Intermediaries

Channel	Number of Agencies	Share (%)	Premium (RMB 100 million)	Share(%)	Fees Income (RMB 100 million)	Share (%)
Bank	85019	57.07	3038.99	68.13	112.73	50.75
Post	17543	11.78	627.85	14.08	21.27	9.58
Railway	462	0.31	2.41	0.05	0.24	0.11
Aviation	2110	1.42	2.80	0.06	1.00	0.45
Vehicle	18049	12.11	328.44	7.36	36.48	16.43
Others	25788	17.31	460.15	10.32	50.39	22.68
Total	148971	100.00	4460.64	100.00	222.11	100.00

Insurance Sales Representatives

By the end of 2009, there were 2.91 million (+13.5% YoY) insurance sales representatives, including 2.58 million (+14.5% YoY) life insurance sales representatives and 329 thousand (+6.5% YoY) property insurance sales representatives.

Foreign Insurance Business

In 2009, the premium of foreign-funded insurance companies reached RMB 45.8 billion (+17.5% YoY), accounting for 4.1% (+0.1% YoY) of the national total. Various types of compensation pay-outs totaled RMB 5.92 billion (+40.2% YoY).

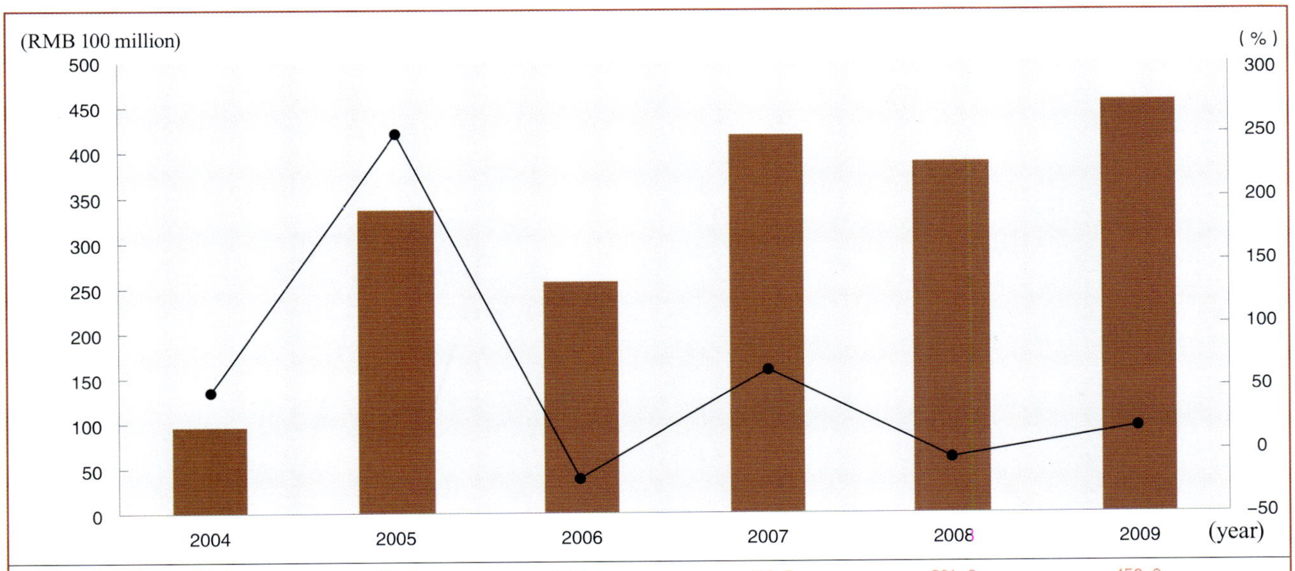

		2004	2005	2006	2007	2008	2009
Premium	(left scale)	97.9	339.3	259.4	420.5	391.2	458.0
Growth rate	(right scale)	45.7	246.3	−23.5	62.1	−7.0	17.5

Figure 8 Premium and Growth Rate of Foreign-funded Insurance Companies during 2004—2009

In 2009, the premium of non-life insurance companies reached RMB 3.18 billion (+10.1% YoY) accounting for 1.1% of the total premium of non-life insurance companies nationwide. The premium from cargo insurance, commercial property insurance and liability insurance made up 74.0% of the foreign non-life insurance business. The compensation pay-outs of foreign-funded non-life insurance companies reached RMB 1.16 billion (+24.7% YoY) and the general expense ratio of the earned premium was 72.5%.

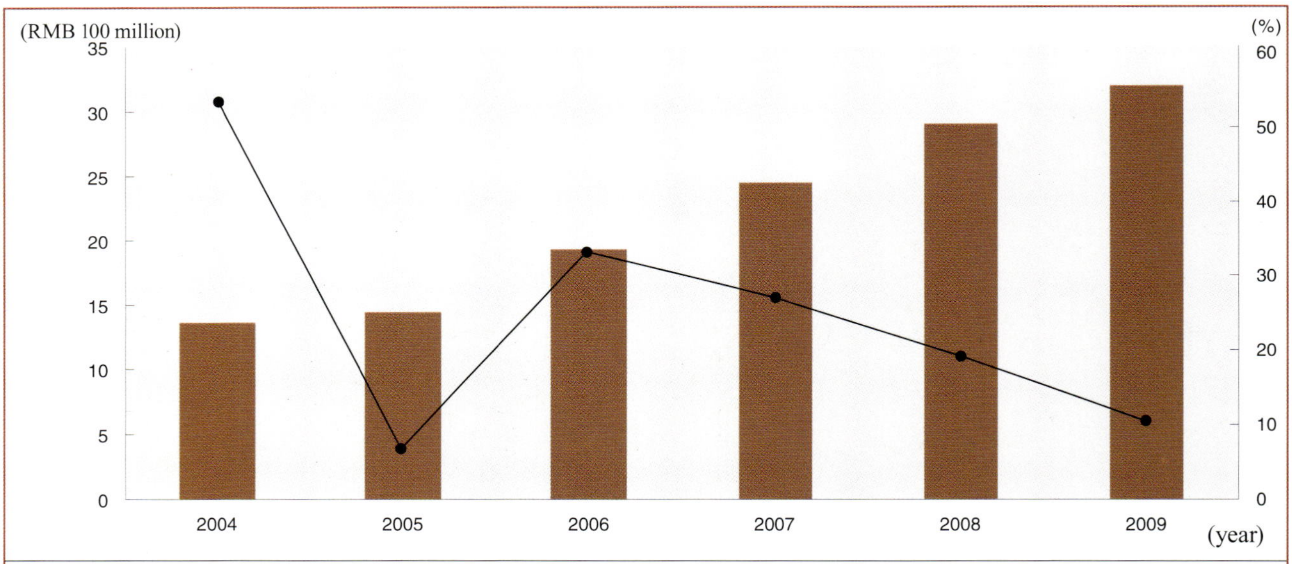

		2004	2005	2006	2007	2008	2009
Premium	(left scale)	13.6	14.5	19.2	24.3	28.9	31.8
Growth rate	(right scale)	52.8	6.7	32.5	26.6	18.8	10.1

Figure 9 Premium and Growth Rate of Foreign-funded Non-life Insurance Companies during 2004–2009

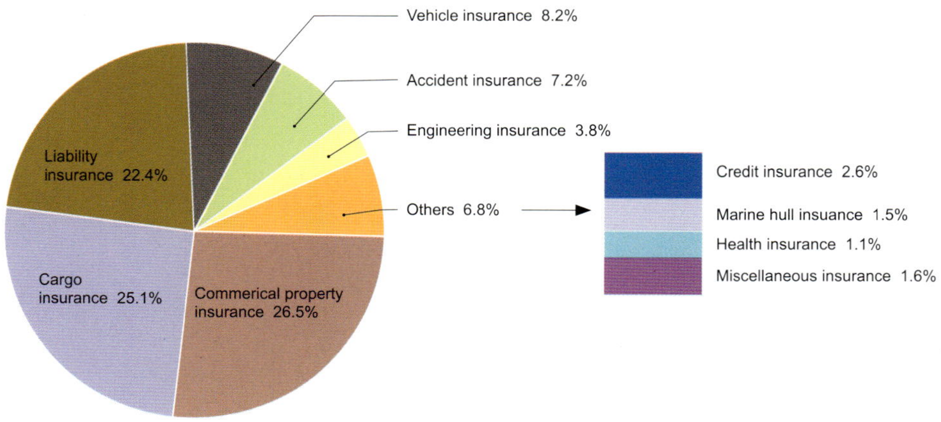

Figure 10 Business Structure of Foreign-funded Non-life Insurance Companies

In 2009, the premium of foreign-funded life insurance companies reached RMB 42.63 billion (+18.1% YoY) accounting for 5.2% of the total premium of the life insurance companies nationwide. New insurance products (including participating products, investment-linked products and universal products) registered a premium of RMB 32.48 billion, representing 76.2% of the total premium of foreign-funded life insurance companies. The compensation pay-outs of foreign-funded life insurance companies reached RMB 4.76 billion (+44.6% YoY)

and the surrender rate was 5.65%.

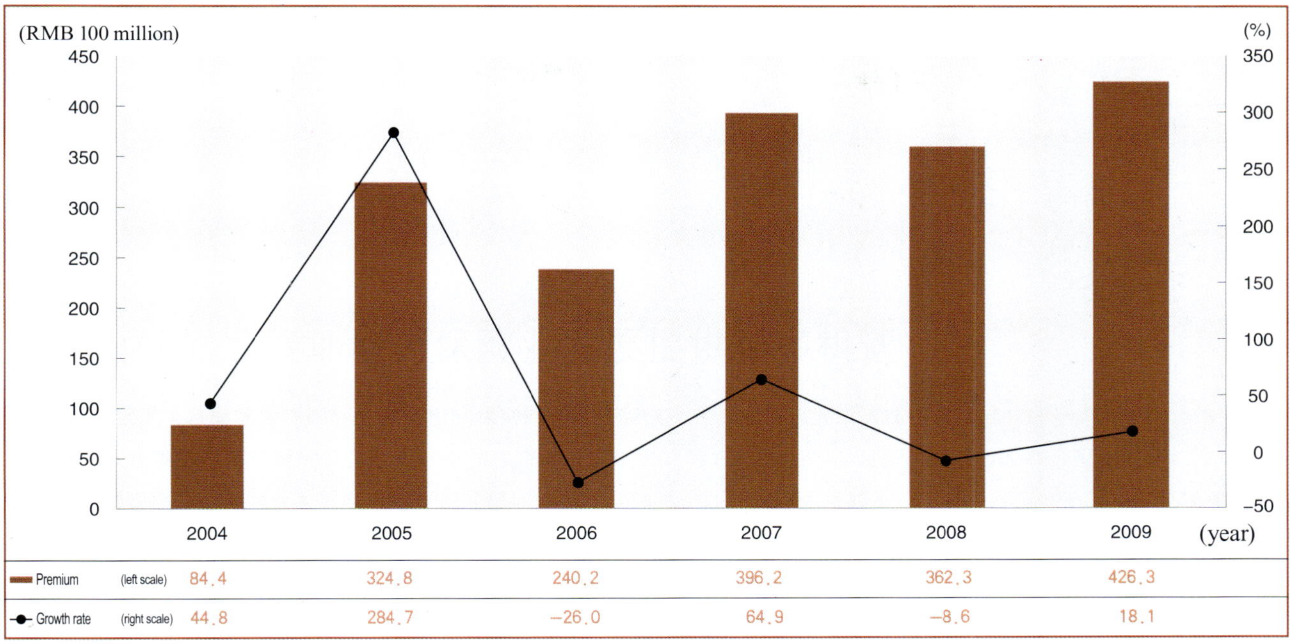

Figure 11　Premium and Growth Rate of Foreign-funded Life Insurance Companies during 2004−2009

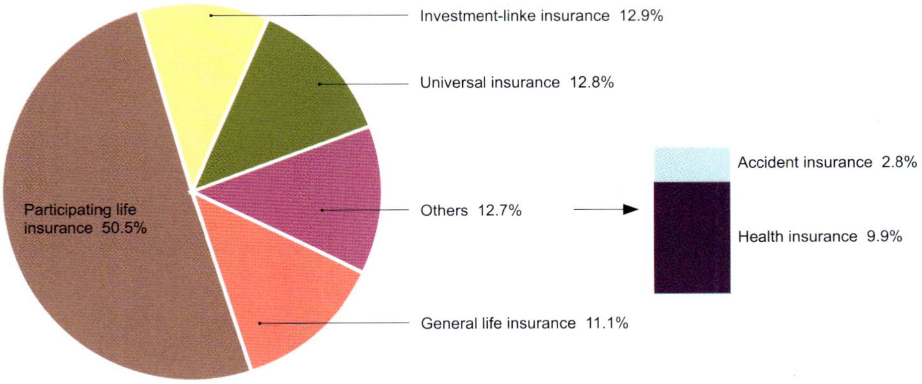

Figure 12　Business Structure of Foreign-funded Life Insurance Companies

The reinsurance premium of foreign-funded reinsurance companies reached RMB 12.36 billion (+81.2% YoY) accounting for 28.5% of the total reinsurance premium of nationwide reinsurance companies and the reinsurance compensation pay-outs totaled RMB 5.24 billion (+62.7% YoY).

By the end of 2009, there were 52 foreign-funded insurance companies consisting of 18 non-life insurance companies, 28 life insurance companies and 6 reinsurance companies. Additionally, two foreign-funded non-life insurance companies and two foreign-funded life insurance companies were newly established in China.

Table 6　Top Five Foreign-funded Non-life Insurance Companies by Market Share①

No.	2009		2008	
	Name	Market Share of Foreign-funded Non-life Insurance Companies (%)	Name	Market Share of Foreign-funded Non-life Insurance Companies (%)
1	AIU	25.5	AIU	29.4
2	Tokio Marine	10.4	Tokio Marine	14.0
3	Mitsui Sumitomo	10.3	Mitsui Sumitomo	10.2
4	Samsung	8.3	Samsung	9.0
5	Allianz	8.1	Allianz	7.5
	Total	62.6	Total	70.1

① The calculation was made according to the premium data of all the companies.

Table 7 Top Five Foreign-funded Life Insurance Companies by Market Share

No	2009		2008	
	Name	Market Share of Foreign-funded Non-life Insurance Companies (%)	Name	Market Share of Foreign-funded Non-life Insurance Companies (%)
1	AIA	18.9	AIA	20.9
2	Cenerali	10.6	Aviva-COFCO	11.0
3	Huatai Life	10.2	CITIC-Prudential	10.3
4	Aviva-COFCO	9.8	Allianz	6.7
5	CITIC-Prudential	9.4	Cenerali	5.8
	Total	58.9	Total	54.7

In 2009, foreign-funded insurance companies still focused their businesses on the earlier opened cities such as Shanghai, Guangzhou, Shenzhen and Beijing. The premium of the foreign-funded insurance companies in the above four cities accounted for 63.4% of foreign premiums of the whole country, down 0.3% on a year-on-year basis.

Table 8 Development of Foreign-funded Insurance Companies in Beijing, Shanghai, Guangzhou and Shenzhen

City	Foreign-funded Insurance Companies			Foreign-funded Non-life Insurance Companies			Foreign-funded Life Insurance Companies		
	Premium (RMB 100mn)	Up YoY (%)	Market share (%)	Premium (RMB 100mn)	Up YoY (%)	Market share (%)	Premium (RMB 100mn)	Up YoY (%)	Market share (%)
Shanghai	112.86	13.19	24.64	13.63	-21.86	42.92	99.23	20.62	23.28
Beijing	100.93	35.31	22.04	4.04	52.58	12.73	96.88	34.68	22.73
Guangzhou	53.61	4.02	11.70	5.02	33.86	15.81	48.59	1.67	11.40
Shenzhen	22.97	2.19	5.02	2.27	5.88	7.16	20.70	1.80	4.86

Insurance Assets Management

The Insurance Industry Kept Developing and the Scale of Capital Utilization Grew Steadily

In the context of proactive fiscal policies and moderately loose monetary policies China's macro economy picked up. The insurance industry posted a continued growing premium, gradually expanding asset scale and further enhanced capital reserves. By the end of 2009, the insurance companies boasted a total asset of RMB 4.1 trillion (+21.6% YoY). The insurance fund application balance reached RMB 3.74 trillion (+22.5% YoY).

Asset Allocation Remained Prudent and Insurance Investment Yielded Good Economic Benefits

The stock market rebounded in volatile trading and the Shanghai Composite Index rose by 80% in 2009 – a result of the recovering national economy and abundant market liquidity. The channels for insurance investment steadily expanded and the categories and scope of investment increased as well. Based on the changes in the external market insurance companies optimized their asset allocation and gradually reduced the proportion of low-interest and long-term bonds to lower the risk of bond depreciation. By increasing the proportion of equity assets according to market trends they achieved good investment returns. In 2009, the return on capital utilization achieved by the insurance companies amounted to RMB 214.17 billion, and the average rate of return was 6.41%.

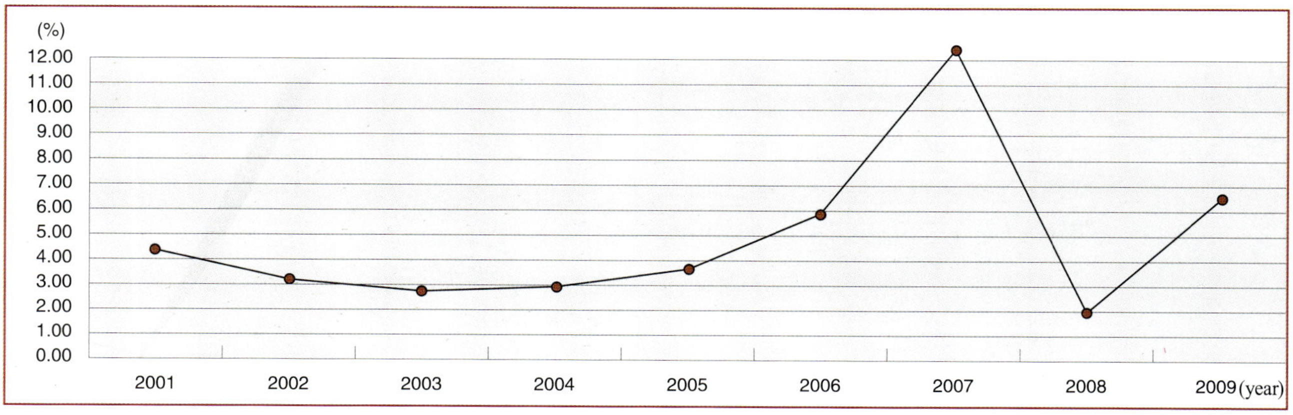

Figure 13 Rate of Return on Investment of the Insurance Companies during 2001–2009

The Insurance Asset Management System Kept Improving and Investment Categories Became More Available in an Orderly Manner

In 2009, the insurance regulator launched a series of regulation documents concerning insurance asset management with a view to deepening the institutional construction and specifying investment regulations and expanding the room for asset allocation. *The Circular on Regulating Stock Investment Businesses of Insurance Institutions*, released in March 2009, further requiring insurance companies to optimize the management of stock asset allocation, enhance dynamic surveillance over market risks and improve independent allocation and investment management capabilities of insurance institutions. *The Circular on the Plans for Insurance Funds' Investment in Infrastructure Bonds* was released to steadily advance the construction of insurance capital-funded infrastructure projects related to transportation, communication and energy and expand the investment channels for insurance institutions. *The Circular on Increasing the Varieties of Bond Investment for Insurance Institutions* was promulgated to adjust the policies regarding bonds investment, increase the varieties of investment and improve asset allocation. The Circular on Strengthening the Management of Bond Repurchase Business of Insurance Institutions issued in August urged insurance companies to improve bond repurchase management systems, intensify the management of capital used for repurchase and guard against risks involved in bond repurchase. *The Circular on Matters Related to the Investment in Unsecured Enterprise Bonds by Insurance Institutions* that debuted in December called for intensified management of unsecured bond investment, standardized investment practices and greater attention to investment risks.

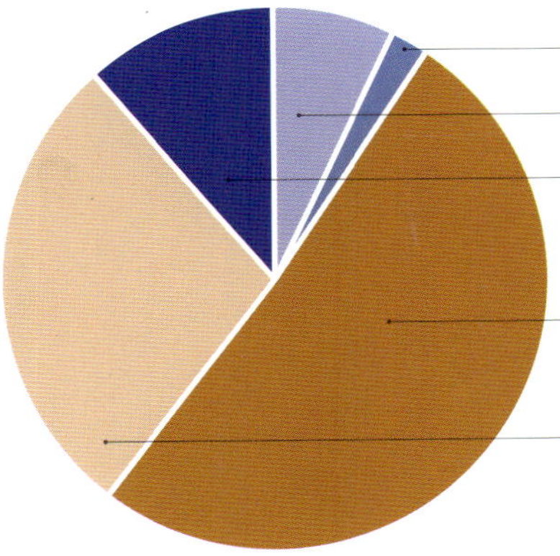

Figure 14 Application Structure of Insurance Funds

Risk Control Involved in Insurance Asset Management Made Headway

In 2009, the insurance regulator further enhanced the risk control of insurance assets by intensifying guidance, adjusting investment policies and formulating criteria for investment management capabilities. *The Circular on Strengthening Risk Control Involved in Insurance Asset Allocation* made public in February 2009 required insurance companies to prevent risks related to product pricing, asset mismatch and interest rates, strengthen risk management of insurance asset allocation and guard against systematic risks. *The Criteria for the Stock Investment Management Capabilities of Insurance Companies and the Criteria for the Credit Risk Management Capabilities of Insurance Institutions* released in March focused on enhanced asset management capabilities, investment risk prevention and asset security.

06

2010 Development Prospects for China's Insurance Market

- The Generally Good Economic Environment Offered More Opportunities for the Development of the Insurance Industry
- The Insurance Industry is Expected to Maintain Fast and Sound Development Amid the Transformation of the Economic Mode

In 2010, China will overcome the adverse effects of the global financial crisis and continue the good momentum of growth. The insurance industry will strive to maintain the fast and sound development by transforming modes of operation, adjusting industrial structure and preventing potential risks.

2010 Development Prospects for China's Insurance Market

The Generally Good Economic Environment Offered More Opportunities for the Development of the Insurance Industry

2010 is a key year in which China continued to tackle the financial crisis, maintain fast and sound economic development and accelerate the transformation of the growth mode. China will further implement proactive fiscal policies and moderately loose monetary policies, pay greater attention to the transformation of its development mode and economic restructuring and further reform the distribution system. The income of both urban and rural residents is expected to improve and the insurance industry may have a better external environment for development. Meanwhile, the further progress in the social security system and medical system reforms paves the way for the expansion of the insurance industry. It is worth noting that although 2010 may see a better environment than 2009, the foundation for China's economic recovery isn't solid enough and extremely complex situations and numerous uncertainties facing the insurance industry raise the bar for risk prevention.

The Insurance Industry is Expected to Maintain Fast and Sound Development Amid the Transformation of the Economic Mode

In 2010, China's insurance industry will take the transformation of economic growth mode as its primary strategic task. By basing steady growth on improving quality, optimizing structure, increasing benefits and enhancing services, the insurance industry will vigorously push for the industrial transformation from homogeneous to differentiated competition and from extensive to intensive resource utilization. With the continuous exploration and innovative development of the insurance industry the insurance market is expected to maintain its fast and healthy development in 2010.

07

Appendix

- Important Regulatory Trends of China's Insurance Market in 2009
- Key Socio-economic Social Indicators of China during 2002–2009
- Key Financial Indicators of China during 2002–2009
- Key Insurance Indicators of China during 2002–2009
- Key Economic and Financial Websites in China

>> Appendix 1

Important Regulatory Trends of China's Insurance Market in 2009

1. The Circular on Strengthening the Administration of Investment-linked Insurance Sales Activities

Released by CIRC on January 23, 2009, the circular was intended to intensify the administration of investment-linked insurance sales. Specifically, it is designed to ensure that the investment-linked insurance is sold by qualified sales persons to the customers with corresponding risk tolerance through proper sales channels, remove possible sources of misguidance, reduce dispute complaints and protect the interests of insurants.

2. Insurance Law of the People's Republic of China [Revised]

The law was revised and passed by the Seventh Session of the Standing Committee of the National People's Congress on February 28, 2009, and implemented as of October 1, 2009. The newly revised law further highlights the protection of the interests of insurants, strengthens insurance surveillance and risk prevention, broadens the fields of insurance services and raises the bar for the lawful operation of insurance institutions.

3. The Code of Conduct of Insurance Regulators and the Code of Conduct of Insurance Practitioners

They were released by CIRC on February 28, 2009. To improve and strengthen the staff working in the insurance industry, the codes specify both the encouraged and forbidden practices for regulators and practitioners, which is of great significance for further improving the overall quality of regulators and practitioners and regulating their professional conduct.

4. The Circular on Regulating the Administration of Policy-guided Agriculture Insurance Businesses

Released by CIRC on April 13, 2009, it further regulates the administration of policy-guided agriculture insurance and is important for protecting the legitimate rights of rural insurants and promoting the steady and healthy development of policy-guided agriculture insurance businesses.

5. Opinions on the Insurance Industry's Further Implementation of the Medical Reform Spirit and Active Participation in the Establishment of a Multi-level Medical Security System

Released by CIRC on May 27, 2009, the opinions were designed to implement *The Opinions on Deepening the Reform in China's Medical and Health System and The Implementation Plan for the Recent Priorities of the Health Care System Reform (2009-2011)* and were launched by the CPC Central Committee and State Council. The opinions also offer important guidelines for the development of commercial health insurance and for stronger engagement in commercial insurance in China's medical security system.

6. The Circular on Further Strengthening Industrial Restructuring, Transforming Mode of Industrial Growth and Promoting the Fast and Sound Development of the Life Insurance Industry

Released on August 2, 2009, it offers guidance on how to define the principles, enrich the connotation and improve the assessment indicators of industrial restructuring. It also helps push forward the multi-layer and all-directional restructuring of the life insurance sector. The circular is of great importance for further increasing awareness of the industrial restructuring and promoting the fast and sound development of the life insurance sector.

7. The Circular on Preventing the Risks Involved in Vehicle Insurance Claim Settlement

Released by CIRC on August 18, 2009, it requires insurance companies to further fortify the construction of the management system for vehicle insurance claim settlement, strictly control risks, improve the quality of services related to vehicle insurance claim settlement and protect the legitimate rights and interests of insurants and victims in road traffic accidents.

8. Rules on the Administration of Insurance Companies

The rules were released by CIRC on September 25, 2009 and implemented as of October 1, 2009. There are of great significance for further improving the means and effects of insurance regulation and promoting the reform of insurance companies' operational and managerial systems. They are expected to help improve the insurance services and better protect the interests of insurance applicants and insurants.

9. Administrative Measures for the Information Disclosure of New-type Personal Insurance Products

The Measures were released by CIRC on September 25, 2009 and implemented as of October 1, 2009. It require information disclosure to be more timely, accurate and transparent. By strengthening the insurance companies' compulsory obligation of information disclosure, they play an important role in regulating the promotion and sales practices of insurance companies and checking sales misguidance.

10. The Provisions on the Regulation of Specialized Insurance Agencies, the Provisions on the Regulation of Insurance Brokers and the Provisions on the Regulation of Surveyors and Loss Adjusters

They were released by CIRC on September 25, 2009 and implemented as of October 1, 2009. The three provisions further improve the insurance intermediary regulation systems, help enhance the quality, management, service and capital capabilities of intermediary institutions and ensure the sustained, steady and healthy development of the insurance intermediary industry.

>>Appendix 2

Key Socio-economic Social Indicators of China during 2002–2009

Table 1 GDP and Structure, 2002–2009

Year	GDP		Primary industry		Secondary industry		Tertiary industry	
	Absolute Value (RMB 100 million)	Growth Rate (%)	Absolute Value (RMB 100 million)	Growth Rate (%)	Absolute Value (RMB 100 million)	Growth Rate (%)	Absolute Value (RMB 100 million)	Growth Rate (%)
2002	120333	9.1	16239	2.9	53897	9.8	50197	10.4
2003	135823	10.0	17069	2.5	62436	12.7	56318	9.5
2004	159878	10.1	20956	6.3	73904	11.1	65018	10.0
2005	182321	9.9	22718	5.2	86208	11.4	73395	9.6
2006	210871	11.1	24737	5.0	103162	13.0	82972	10.8
2007	249530	11.9	28095	3.7	121381	13.4	100054	12.6
2008	300670	9.0	34000	5.5	146183	9.3	120487	9.5
2009	335353	8.7	35477	4.2	156958	9.5	142918	8.9

Note: Source: China Statistical Yearbook 2009 and Statistical Communiqué 2009 by the National Bureau of Statistics of China.

Table 2 Total Population, Birth Rate and Natural Growth Rate, year-end 2002–2009

Year	Year-end Total Population (10000)	Birth Rate (‰)	Natural Growth Rate (‰)
2002	128453	12.86	6.45
2003	129227	12.41	6.01
2004	129988	12.29	5.87
2005	130756	12.40	5.89
2006	131448	12.09	5.28
2007	132129	12.10	5.17
2008	132802	12.14	5.08
2009	133474	12.13	5.05

Note: Source: China Statistical Yearbook 2009 and Statistical Communiqué 2009 by the National Bureau of Statistics of China.

Table 3 Number of Registered Urban Unemployed Persons and Registered Urban Unemployment Rate, 2002–2009

Year	Number of Registered Urban Unemployed Persons (10000)	Registered Urban Unemployment Rate (%)
2002	770	4.0
2003	800	4.3
2004	827	4.2
2005	839	4.2
2006	847	4.1
2007	830	4.0
2008	886	4.2
2009	921	4.3

Note: Source: China Statistical Yearbook 2009 and Statistical Communiqué 2009 by the National Bureau of Statistics of China.

Table 4 Per Capita Net Income of Rural Households and Per Capita Disposable Income of Urban Households, 2002–2009

Year	Per Capita Net Income of Rural Households		Per Capita Disposable Income of Urban Households	
	Absolute Value（RMB）	Growth Rate（%）	Absolute Value（RMB）	Growth Rate（%）
2002	2476	4.8	7703	13.4
2003	2622	4.3	8472	9.0
2004	2936	6.8	9422	7.7
2005	3255	6.2	10493	9.6
2006	3587	7.4	11759	10.4
2007	4140	9.5	13786	12.2
2008	4761	8.0	15781	8.4
2009	5153	8.5	17175	9.8

Note: Source: China Statistical Yearbook 2009 and Statistical Communiqué 2009 by the National Bureau of Statistics of China.

Table 5 Total Social Fixed Asset Investment, 2002–2009

Year	Total Social Fixed Asset Investment（RMB 100 million）	Growth Rate（%）
2002	43500	16.9
2003	55567	27.7
2004	70477	26.6
2005	88604	25.7
2006	109870	24.0
2007	137239	24.8
2008	172291	25.5
2009	224846	30.1

Note: Source: China Statistical Yearbook 2009 and Statistical Communiqué 2009 by the National Bureau of Statistics of China.

Table 6 Consumer Price Index and Price Index of Fixed Asset Investment, 2002–2009

Year	Consumer Price Index（index of previous year =100）	Price Index of Fixed Asset Investment（index of previous year =100）
2002	99.2	100.2
2003	101.2	102.2
2004	103.9	105.6
2005	101.8	101.6
2006	101.5	101.5
2007	106.4	105.5
2008	105.9	108.9
2009	99.3	97.6

Note: Source: China Statistical Yearbook 2009 and Statistical Communiqué 2009 by the National Bureau of Statistics of China.

Table 7 Total Volume of Foreign Trade, 2002–2009

Year	Total Volume of Foreign Trade (USD 100 million)	Growth Rate (%)
2002	6208	21.8
2003	8512	37.1
2004	11548	35.7
2005	14221	23.2
2006	17607	23.8
2007	21738	23.5
2008	25616	17.8
2009	22072	-13.9

Note: Source: Statistical Communiqué by the National Bureau of Statistics of China.

Table 8 Total Fiscal Expenditure, 2002–2009

Year	Total Fiscal Revenue (RMB 100 million)	Growth Rate (%)	Total Fiscal Expenditure (RMB 100 million)	Growth Rate (%)
2002	18903.64	15.4	22053.15	16.7
2003	21715.25	14.9	24649.95	11.8
2004	26396.47	21.6	28486.89	15.6
2005	31649.29	19.9	33930.28	19.1
2006	38760.20	22.5	40422.73	19.1
2007	51321.78	32.4	49781.35	23.2
2008	61330.35	19.5	62592.66	25.7
2009	68476.88	11.7	75873.64	21.2

Note: Source: China Statistical Yearbook 2009 and Statistical Communiqué 2009 by the National Bureau of Statistics of China.

>>Appendix 3

Key Financial Indicators of China during 2002–2009

Table 1 Deposits Balance of National Urban and Rural Residents, 2002–2009

Year	Deposits Balance of National Urban and Rural Residents (RMB 100 million)	Annual Increase (RMB 100 million)
2002	86911	13233
2003	103617	16632
2004	119555	15929
2005	141051	21497
2006	161587	20544
2007	172534	10947
2008	217885	45351
2009	260772	42887

Note: Source: China Statistical Yearbook 2009 and Statistical Communiqué 2009 by the National Bureau of Statistics of China.

Table 2 Number of Listed Companies, Shares Issued, Capital Raised, 2002–2009

Year	Number of Listed Companies	Amount Issued (100 million shares)	Raised Capital of Shares (RMB 100 million)
2002	1224	291.74	961.75
2003	1287	281.43	1357.75
2004	1377	227.92	1510.94
2005	1381	567.05	1882.51
2006	1434	1287.77	5594.29
2007	1550	637.24	8680.17
2008	1625	180.29	3852.21
2009	1718	–	–

Note: Source: China Statistical Yearbook 2009 and Statistical Communiqué 2009 by the National Bureau of Statistics of China.

Table 3 Gold Reserve and Foreign Exchange Reserve, 2002–2009

Year	Gold Reserve (10000 ounce)	Foreign Exchange Reserve (USD 100 million)
2002	1929	2864.07
2003	1929	4032.51
2004	1929	6099.32
2005	1929	8188.72
2006	1929	10663.40
2007	1929	15282.49
2008	1929	19460.30
2009	3389	23991.52

Note: Source: China Statistical Yearbook 2009 and website of the People's Bank of China (www.pbc.gov.cn).

Table 4 Annual Exchange Rate, 2002–2009

Year	USD: RMB (ending balance)	USD: RMB (average)
2002	8.2773	8.2769
2003	8.2767	8.2770
2004	8.2765	8.2768
2005	8.0702	8.1949
2006	7.8087	7.9735
2007	7.3046	7.3676
2008	6.8346	6.8424
2009	6.8282	6.8279

Note: Source: Website of the People's Bank of China (www.pbc.gov.cn).

>>Appendix 4

Key Insurance Indicators of China during 2002–2009

Table 1 Distribution of Premium, 2002–2009

Year	Insurance Premium		Life Insurance Companies		Non-life Insurance Companies	
	Absolute Value (RMB 100 million)	Growth Rate (%)	Absolute Value (RMB 100 million)	Growth Rate (%)	Absolute Value (RMB 100 million)	Growth Rate (%)
2002	3048.3	44.1	2275.1	59.7	773.2	11.9
2003	3848.8	26.3	2983.2	31.1	865.6	12.0
2004	4323.0	12.3	3198.2	7.2	1124.8	30.0
2005	4928.4	14.0	3644.9	14.0	1283.1	14.1
2006	5640.2	14.4	4059.1	11.3	1581.1	23.2
2007	7033.4	25.0	4946.5	21.9	2086.6	32.0
2008	9789.1	39.2	7342.6	48.5	2446.2	17.3
2009	11137.3	13.8	8144.2	11.0	2992.9	22.4

Table 2 Distribution of Premium by Region in 2009

Region	Insurance Premium			Property Insurance			Life Insurance		
	Accumulative (RMB 10000)	YoY Growth (%)	Proportion (%)	Accumulative (RMB 10000)	YoY Growth (%)	Proportion (%)	Accumulative (RMB 10000)	YoY Growth (%)	Proportion (%)
Total National Insurance Premium	111372989.22	13.83	100.00	28758335.46	23.09	100.00	82614653.76	10.93	100.00
1. Independent Business Income of Headquarters	251913.64	68.09	0.23	244835.44	99.06	0.85	7078.20	−69.81	0.01
2. East Region	65178625.17	13.36	58.52	17339672.08	20.81	60.29	47838953.09	10.88	57.91
Beijing	6975952.11	19.05	6.26	1644197.29	22.57	5.72	5331754.82	18.01	6.45
Tianjin	1512872.70	−13.86	1.36	457959.19	9.51	1.59	1054913.51	−21.16	1.28
Hebei	6010863.64	25.07	5.40	1286741.63	24.75	4.47	4724122.01	25.15	5.72
Liaoning	3454932.62	5.10	3.10	864687.09	27.28	3.01	2590245.53	−0.68	3.14
Dalian	1163310.58	8.28	1.04	328789.23	20.46	1.14	834521.35	4.14	1.01
Shanghai	6650258.77	10.83	5.97	1518069.76	15.19	5.28	5132189.01	9.60	6.21
Jiangsu	9077307.31	17.06	8.15	2283865.88	26.10	7.94	6793441.43	14.31	8.22
Zhejiang	5380952.46	9.98	4.83	1963373.42	20.42	6.83	3417579.04	4.77	4.14
Ningbo	1074435.32	23.35	0.96	510768.02	26.61	1.78	563667.30	20.53	0.68
Fujian	2722579.82	11.67	2.44	726691.12	17.85	2.53	1995888.70	9.58	2.42
Xiamen	583933.42	24.57	0.52	194160.09	24.43	0.68	389773.33	24.65	0.47
Shandong	6775768.68	18.61	6.08	1736748.71	27.78	6.04	5039019.98	15.75	6.10
Qingdao	1153100.85	12.25	1.04	343380.04	21.27	1.19	809720.81	8.82	0.98
Guangdong	9595713.73	8.53	8.62	2391023.09	15.08	8.31	7204690.65	6.52	8.72
Shenzhen	2715944.75	12.78	2.44	970684.25	14.41	3.38	1745260.50	11.89	2.11
Hainan	330698.40	9.99	0.30	118533.28	12.96	0.41	212165.13	8.40	0.26

continue

Region	Insurance Premium			Property Insurance			Life Insurance		
	Accumulative (RMB 10000)	YoY Growth (%)	Proportion (%)	Accumulative (RMB 10000)	YoY Growth (%)	Proportion (%)	Accumulative (RMB 10000)	YoY Growth (%)	Proportion (%)
3. Middle Region	25830975.09	12.92	23.19	5377037.52	24.43	18.70	20453937.57	10.24	24.76
Shanxi	2892494.53	10.87	2.60	671258.36	11.70	2.33	2221236.17	10.62	2.69
Jilin	1848668.86	16.33	1.66	404585.90	25.55	1.41	1444082.96	13.98	1.75
Heilongjiang	2783743.02	10.82	2.50	567223.28	18.29	1.97	2216519.74	9.06	2.68
Anhui	3572103.89	20.46	3.21	875885.04	36.95	3.05	2696218.85	15.93	3.26
Jiangxi	1871351.38	9.21	1.68	441298.59	31.90	1.53	1430052.79	3.70	1.73
Henan	5653913.96	8.95	5.08	977354.13	25.54	3.40	4676559.83	6.03	5.66
Hebei	3724234.43	17.43	3.34	689729.65	25.43	2.40	3034504.78	15.75	3.67
Hunan	3484465.02	11.51	3.13	749702.58	21.67	2.61	2734762.45	9.01	3.31
4. West Region	20111475.30	16.12	18.06	5796790.41	26.93	20.16	14314684.89	12.25	17.33
Chongqing	2447045.41	22.02	2.20	470583.98	24.64	1.64	1976461.43	21.41	2.39
Sichuan	5790282.92	17.15	5.20	1487178.89	35.50	5.17	4303104.03	11.91	5.21
Guizhou	952286.64	19.10	0.86	360529.34	26.14	1.25	591757.30	15.19	0.72
Yunnan	1800824.56	8.88	1.62	681665.27	23.48	2.37	1119159.29	1.57	1.35
Tibet	40141.73	23.48	0.04	34250.11	19.60	0.12	5891.62	52.25	0.01
Shaanxi	2595947.64	19.20	2.33	605288.30	30.82	2.10	1990659.35	16.07	2.41
Gansu	1143842.26	17.38	1.03	270537.53	19.63	0.94	873304.73	16.70	1.06
Qinghai	182081.85	29.08	0.16	79624.38	26.85	0.28	102457.47	30.87	0.12
Ningxia	392775.13	23.55	0.35	118414.47	24.97	0.41	274360.66	22.95	0.33
Xinjiang	1566941.66	2.74	1.41	518242.23	17.11	1.80	1048699.42	-3.13	1.27
Inner Mongolia	1713104.21	21.20	1.54	673405.08	25.65	2.34	1039699.12	18.48	1.26
Guangxi	1486201.29	11.34	1.33	497070.82	24.13	1.73	989130.47	5.86	1.20

Note: The premiums in various regions and the national total contained in the table were business statistical data.

Table 3 Insurance Penetration and Insurance Density, 2002–2009

Year	Insurance Penetration (%)	Insurance Density (RMB per person)
2002	2.98	237.64
2003	3.33	287.44
2004	3.39	332.16
2005	2.70	375.64
2006	2.80	431.30
2007	2.93	532.42
2008	3.25	736.74
2009	3.32	834.41

Table 4 Insurance Funds Utilization Yield 2002–2009

Year	Funds Utilization Yield（%）
2002	3.14
2003	2.68
2004	2.87
2005	3.60
2006	5.80
2007	12.17
2008	1.91
2009	6.41

Table 5 List of Asset Management Companies in 2009

Rank	Name
1	PICC Asset Management Company Limited
2	China Life Asset Management Company Limited
3	China Reinsurance (Group) Corporation
4	PingAn Asset Management Co., Ltd.
5	Huatai Asset Management Company Ltd.
6	Taikang Asset Management Co., Ltd.
7	New China Asset Management Co., Ltd.
8	Pacific Asset Management Co., Ltd.
9	Taiping Asset Management Co., Ltd.

Table 6 Top Ten Insurance Brokers by Brokerage in 2009

Rank	Name	Business Income (RMB 10000)	Market Share（%）
1	Chang´an Insurance Brokers Co., Ltd.	40774.66	12.32
2	Beijing Union Insurance Broker Co., Ltd.	24999.49	7.55
3	Aon-COFCO Insurance Brokers Co., Ltd.	18080.71	5.46
4	Jiang Tai Insurance Broker Co., Ltd.	17765.79	5.37
5	Willis Insurance Brokers Co., Ltd	15765.96	4.76
6	Marsh (Beijing) Insurance Brokers Co., Ltd.	13553.44	4.09
7	Jingsheng Insurance Brokers Co., Ltd.	10648.96	3.22
8	Huatai Insurance Agency & Consultant Service Ltd.	8998.31	2.72
9	Air Union Insurance Brokers Co., Ltd.	8065.86	2.44
10	Chang Cheng Insurance Brokers Ltd.	7931.44	2.40

Table 7 Top Ten Insurance Agents by Agency Income in 2009

Rank	Name	Business Income (RMB 10000)	Market Share (%)
1	Hunan Post Insurance Agency Co., Ltd.	14306.00	3.19
2	Guangzhou Fanhua Yi′an Insurance Agency Co., Ltd.	9989.11	2.23
3	Dongguan Nanfengjiayu Insurance Agency Co., Ltd.	9148.14	2.04
4	Guangzhou Nanfeng Insurance Agency Co., Ltd.	9127.86	2.04
5	Hebei Shengan Insurance Agency Co., Ltd.	8824.13	1.97
6	Sichuan CNINSURE Agency Co., Ltd.	7039.52	1.57
7	Shandong Huakang Insurance Agency Co., Ltd.	6418.18	1.43
8	Guangzhou Huixin Insurance Agency Co., Ltd.	6117.19	1.36
9	Hubei Huakang Insurance Agency Co., Ltd.	5662.94	1.26
10	Jiangsu Huakang Insurance Agency Co., Ltd.	5480.96	1.22

Table 8 Top Ten Insurance Surveyors and Loss Adjusters Companies by Business Income in 2009

Rank	Name	Business Income (RMB 10000)	Market Share (%)
1	Shenzhen Mintai′an Insurance Surveyors & Loss Adjusters Co., Ltd.	19719.26	17.44
2	CNINSURE INC.	9052.64	8.00
3	Shenzhen Zhixinda Insurance Surveyors & Loss Adjusters Co., Ltd.	3666.29	3.24
4	Shanghai Teamhead Surveyors Co., Ltd.	3658.37	3.23
5	Shenzhen Liansheng Insurance Surveyors & Loss Adjusters Co., Ltd.	3645.28	3.22
6	Guangzhou Tianxin Insurance Surveyors & Loss Adjusters Co., Ltd.	3613.23	3.19
7	Shanghai Highlevels Surveying Co., Ltd.	3377.96	2.99
8	Guangdong Henglianghang Insurance Surveyors & Loss Adjusters Co., Ltd.	3213.11	2.84
9	Jingsheng Insurance Surveyors & Loss Adjusters Co., Ltd.	2947.92	2.61
10	GAB Robins China Ltd.	2915.88	2.58

>>Appendix 5

Key Economic and Financial Websites in China

The People's Bank of China http://www.pbc.gov.cn
China Banking Regulatory Commission http://www.cbrc.gov.cn
China Securities Regulatory Commission http://www.csrc.gov.cn
China Insurance Regulatory Commission http://www.circ.gov.cn
National Development and Reform Commission http://www.ndrc.gov.cn
Ministry of Finance People's Republic of China http://www.mof.gov.cn
Ministry of Human Resources and Social Security of the People's Republic of China http://www.mohrss.gov.cn
National Bureau of Statistics of China http://www.stats.gov.cn

图书在版编目（CIP）数据

2009中国保险市场年报（2009 Zhongguo Baoxian Shichang Nianbao）/中国保险监督管理委员会编．—北京：中国金融出版社，2010.9
ISBN 978-7-5049-5636-1

Ⅰ.①2… Ⅱ.①中… Ⅲ.①保险业—市场—研究报告—中国—2009
Ⅳ.①F842.6

中国版本图书馆CIP数据核字(2010)第169124号

出版
发行 中国金融出版社
社址 北京市丰台区益泽路2号
市场开发部 (010)63272190，66070804（传真）
网上书店 http://www.chinafph.com (010)63286832，63365686（传真）
读者服务部 (010)66070833，62568380
邮编 100071
经销 新华书店
印刷 北京松源印刷有限公司
尺寸 210毫米×296毫米
印张 5.25
字数 142千
版次 2010年9月第1版
印次 2010年9月第1次印刷
定价 90.00元
ISBN 978-7-5049-5636-1/F.5196
如出现印装错误本社负责调换 联系电话：(010)63263947